Joined Writing

An anthology of writings by members of the Barmouth University of the Third Age

Editor-in-Chief
Richard Paramor

ROUND HOUSE PUBLISHING

Our thanks

The production of this anthology has been made possible through the encouragement and generous financial support of the Communities First Tr Fund, and the Wales Council for Voluntary Action.

Help and guidance from Communities First Barmouth, and Age Concern Cymru has been invaluable.

Published December 2008

ISBN 978-0-9560394-0-8

Published by
Round House Publishing
Dolgellau, Gwynedd, LL40 1LD

Cover illustration from an original watercolour by
Glenys Lawson

Page illustrations by
Jack Richardson

Round House Publishing logo designed by
David Rowley

Printed by
Barmouth Printers
Park Road, Barmouth, Gwynedd, LL42 1PH

troduction

ing the summer of 2007, a group of enthusiastic writers formed a writers'
ıp as part of the newly established Barmouth branch of the University of the
d Age. Styles of writing, skills and experience varied considerably amongst
members of the group, but one common thread that wove its way through
band of diverse wordsmiths was a determination to write as interestingly,
entertainingly as possible; to share openly, criticisms and praises alike; and
ıjoy to the utmost the delights of setting words on paper.

decision to put together this anthology was borne from a wish, modestly
en, to share our writings with others; a fancy to bring some entertainment
t amusing, macabre or even soul-searching) to those with patience to read
words, and – we admit – an egotistical desire to see our efforts in print.

y member of the group has contributed to this book, in which we offer you
selection of poetry and prose - and several bits-and-pieces that fall into
ıer of the categories. Modest though they might be, they are our own.

e writers

order in which the items in the book appear bears no relationship to the
, standing, or reputation of the writers concerned. Lots were drawn to
le in which order the writers should appear, and brief information about
writers appears before their work.

contributors to this anthology are:

e artists

only are all the writers of this anthology members of the Barmouth
ersity of the Third Age, but so are the artists who have produced all the
rations – the cover, the interior drawings, and our logo.

ROUND HOUSE PUBLISHING

hn Reece

*n in a workhouse in Tetbury, Gloucester, John was adopted at the age of
months by a Herefordshire family, and spent his childhood and early adult
rs in Ross-on-Wye. He was educated at Ross Grammar School. John and
late wife adopted four children – including twin-boys, and he has six
ndchildren. Much of his career was spent in the publishing industry where
worked with Victor Gollancz, and Michael Joseph as a publishers agent,
cing after many notable authors including Daphne Du Maurier, Spike
ligan, Wynford Vaughan Thomas, and Dick Francis. Despite these early
s in publishing, he himself had to be brought, screaming, into writing, and
only picked up a pen in recent times. Although long since retired, John is
rently heavily involved with the work of the British Red Cross.*

1
La Grande Sorpressa
(The big surprise)

awn was breaking over the ancient oaks of the Royal Forest of Dean; oaks,
which, in the fifteenth century, would have been felled to build warships
Henry VIII. But it wasn't trees or royalty I had on my mind that morning as
zed out of my bedroom window; it was one of the most beautiful women in
world.

rvous excitement was keeping me from sleep. It made sense to get up to
disturbing my wife - and I did have to be at my office in London for 8.30.
breakfasted, and prepared for my day, I kissed Ann goodbye, and joked that
ght never return. That day I was to be minder, and general dogsbody to
ia Loren, and we were both, at the age of forty-five, in the prime of life.
as to meet Miss Loren at London's Ritz Hotel with a chauffer-driven Rolls.
vere off to Birmingham for the day, where our hectic schedule included a
interview, a television appearance, and a book signing session.
ss Loren was waiting for me in the reception lounge and, no doubt
ading to put me at my ease, immediately threw her arms around me and
pered into my ear,
ase John, you must call me Sophia'.
me at my ease be damned, I nearly wet myself; how would I get through
ay? I'd looked after famous authors, politicians, and actors before, but
r someone like this. Already I felt overwhelmed; would it all be too much
e!
ntangling myself from her arms, I guided her to the Rolls and we set off.
ent well until we were about forty miles or so along the M1. A traffic jam

appeared to go all the way to the north of England. We sat for a few minutes what should we do, we had a schedule to keep and the day had hardly started But Charles, our driver, was used to such quandaries, so when a police car sp by on the hard shoulder with blue lights flashing and sirens blaring, he pulled out and, with foot hard down, followed it until it came to a halt where an incident had occurred.

The police driver walked towards us. That's it, I thought, our day's ended before it's begun. After speaking to our driver for a moment or two, the policeman walked up to our window, peered inside, saluted, and wishing us a pleasant day, waved us on. Thank goodness for the British Bobby.

We arrived first at the studios of BRMB, the Birmingham local radio station where the car was immediately surrounded by hordes of screaming people some just gawking, other with autograph books or scraps of paper for Sophia autograph, who although no longer in her acting prime was remembered with affection for her many earlier films. I grabbed her hand, and, with apologies the crowd, we pushed our way through to the dingy staircase leading to the cramped reception area - they probably have wonderful studios in the subur now, but in 1979 they were in upstairs offices at the rough end of Corporation Street. We were offered tea and waited patiently until Sophia was collected f her interview.

'You must come along too,' she said to me, 'I don't like being on my own.'

The studio being very small, with hardly room for two people let alone thre this request caused a problem, but we squeezed in - me sitting next to Sophia swear if we'd got any closer I would have been sitting on her lap, or she on mine!

The interview went without mishap, although she did grasp my hand tightly when the interviewer started asking about her childhood,

'I don't like to talk about that,' she said, 'perhaps your listeners had better the book'.

There's salesmanship I thought.

Fifteen minutes later with the interview over, it was time to leave, but now could spent a while with the excited crowd, and Sophia could sign some autographs and chat to a few people. Then, although only about ten minute walk away, it was back to the car, and off to Rackham's top floor restaurar where I knew, from experience with other authors, we would be well looke after. Again we were inundated with gawpers and autograph hunters, but steered her through to the private screened area where we enjoyed a quie lunch.

It was at this point that my managing director appeared, and, trying to get on the act, apologised for the not personally looking after Sophia earlier in day.

ever mind; Mr Reece is doing a good job, he's looks after me so well that
n the Mafia would be proud, and I would like him to stay with me'.
ith tail between his legs, and directing daggers at me, my boss left us.

was now time to dash to the BBC studios for 'Pebble Mill at One', a daily
gramme of interviews and current affairs reports. Within fifteen minutes we
e at Pebble Mill Studios where the ambience was much more as one would
ect for a star of Sophia's class and a bottle of champagne was opened at
e. Sophia refused, but insisted I should take a glass - who was I to refuse the
hes of this beautiful woman?
ith finishing touches made to hair and makeup, Sophia was invited into the
lio from where the programme would be broadcast live. Again she insisted
t I accompany her. I tried to refuse, but she insisted. Thank goodness she
n't want to hold my hand throughout her appearance, and didn't mind my
ig partially hidden behind some artificial pot plants. She relaxed, and the
rview went well.
ter a few minutes respite in the green room, we were back in the car heading
ards the city centre for two hours of book signings at Hudsons Bookshop, at
 time one of the biggest in Britain.
proaching New Street I was alarmed to see it jammed with people being
trolled, not very effectively, by two mounted police officers. Charles knew
ningham well, and nipped deftly to Hudson's back entrance in Stevenson
e, approached by a passageway underneath the Midland Hotel. I was
arrassed to take Sophia in the goods lift, but there was John Hudson
ing for us.
hink we'd better go straight to the sales floor as there's almost a riot going
ip there, and we've already had one window smashed by people pressing
nst it.'
owds by the score stood around tables piled high with books ready to be
ed. At once, Sophia sat down and started signing; oh, what a professional,
ng what name was to be written inside, and occasionally jumping up and
ging, sometimes even kissing, the customers. We're going to be here all day,
ought, but soon the two hours were up; John Hudson closed the department
rs, and we all sighed with relief. We checked how many books Sophia had
ed; I couldn't believe it – six hundred and thirty, plus another fifty for
omers to collect later! I'd attended many similar events, but had never
re known as many books as that to be signed in so short a time.
n Hudson insisted that Sophia deserved a glass of wine, which this time
accepted, before 'goodbyes' were said with lots more hugs, kisses and
ed autographs for the staff. We retraced our way in the goods lift to the car,
 around the corner to the Midland Hotel, where I had reserved a suite for a
le of hours, so that Sophia could have a rest before our return journey to
lon.

But there he was again, my damned boss putting his oar in, and trying to st[e]
my thunder.

'Let me take you to the suite we have ready for you'

But Sophia would have none of it,

'No, John looks after me very well, we got to know each other today very
nicely, but with you, we don't know each other at all; I think I finish off the d[ay]
with him if you don't mind'.

I could have hugged her.

We were taken to what, it transpired, was the honeymoon suite. Showing u[s]
into the suite, the manager asked what he could fetch us; we suggested a pot [of]
tea with a few sandwiches and cakes. Sophia went into the bedroom, slipped [off]
her shoes, loosened her dress and threw herself, with a sleepy sigh, onto th[e]
four-poster bed.

Soon I heard voices in the corridor, and banging on the door. I went t[o]
investigate the fuss, but it was only hotel staff wanting autographs. I aske[d]
them to leave us alone as Miss Loren wanted to rest, and they obligingly mo[ved]
away at once. But I was concerned that there would be no peace, so suggeste[d I]
should sit outside the door, to keep the fans away whilst she slept. Sophia sa[id]

'No, I want you here with me,'

'OK, I'll sit inside the door then,'

'No, I want you here,'

She was patting the bed; I sat at her side with no small degree of pride.

'John, I've been with you for eight hours, we've chatted a lot, I know how th[e]
land is lying, I know I am feeling safe with you, I want you here next to me a[nd]
I want you to hug me in your arms, because at the moment I feel tired, and [I feel]
very lonely.'

The refreshments arrived at that moment, and saved my falling off the bed [in]
astonishment. I poured the tea and handed her some food, then sat back on [the]
bed. She drank her tea, we hugged, and she fell into a deep sleep while I la[y]
beside her – a bag of nerves.

Three quarters of an hour or so later she awoke, gave me another hug and s[aid]
it was time we set off for London. I telephoned reception; they contacte[d]
Charles, and the car was soon at the back of the hotel.

As she said her 'goodbyes' to the hotel staff and the manager, I noticed her [give]
the manager an envelope which, no doubt, contained a more-than-generous [tip.]

We made an uneventful three-hour journey back to the Ritz Hotel, and [I]
handed over my charge to the manager. She gave me another kiss, and than[ked]
me for taking good care of her.

'I do hope we meet again,' she said, 'but in the meantime enjoy your life.'

Arriving home at midnight, tired but contented, I was greeted by Ann.

'What sort of day have you had?'

'Oh the usual, everything went quite well.'

saw you on Pebble Mill, so at least I know you were where you said you
ıld be.'

ıe moon shone over the ancient forest oaks as I crept into bed, tired, but
tented with a job well done.

Hudsons Bookshops

Hudsons Bookshops Limited

A Pentos Company

116 New Street, Birmingham B2 4JJ, England
Telephone: 021-643 8311
Telex: 337001

Our ref: JH:BCP

Your ref:

Mr. J. Reece,
Hillsborough,
The Avenue,
Ross on Wye,
Herefordshire. HR9 5AW.

30 March 1979

Dear John,

Just a short note to thank you for all the work you did before,
during and after Sophia Loren's visit to Birmingham. It was
the most successful signing session but above all it certainly
was the happiest that I can recall and once again my sincerest
thanks.

With best wishes and kindest regards,

Yours sincerely,

John Hudson

John Hudson.

Registered Office: As above.
VAT Registration No. 109 9266 49
Registered in England No. 216843

2
To the Beach in Odd Wellies

Her letter was dated 1967. She thanked me for my earlier letter, and wro 'if you turn up about four o'clock on Wednesday 19th you will find m thinking of putting the kettle on!' She went on to tell me that she had beer working hard during the past months and had finished her biography of th early days of the Bacon brothers, Francis and Anthony, entitled 'Golden Lad The letter finished quite formally, 'Yours sincerely......'

Thus, at about half past three on a sunny afternoon in the middle of June, was twisting my way around narrow Cornish lanes. It was a beautiful day wit the hedgerows full of the remaining spring flowers, and the buds of summe ready to burst open.

It was difficult to see over the high banked roadside with it's closely kni hedgerows but I knew that the house I was looking for was somewhere in th vicinity.

Suddenly the road, the banks, and the hedges became level, and I reached t rather faded and dilapidated gate at the entrance to a long drive that wound way to the 'big' house. The drive looked as if to go on for miles and miles, wi large expanse of woodland at the end, and the blue of the sea beyond. As approach the woodland I could see the chimney pots of the house poking th noses above the trees.

Very nervously, I approached the huge, unpainted oak door; this was, after my first assignment with one of the most famous authors of her generation, who had many novels, biographies and travel books to her name. What's m my career in publishing, and with the publishing house in question, was sti barely in its sixth month. I knew about selling books to bookshops and libraries, but had little experience of authors; least of all highly respected on

My publishing house had asked me to call on this person, who had bee somewhat of a recluse over recent years, to persuade her to visit London t discuss her next title. I was also to encourage her to make some public appearances with book signings, literary lunches, and radio and televisio interviews; but I had been warned to tread lightly as she was very touchy ab such things.

I was worrying needlessly; the door was opened by a tall, untidily dresse grey-haired lady whose beautiful welcoming smile put me at ease at once.

'Oh, hello, you must be Mr Reece, may I call you John? Do come in, and pl excuse the wellies, I was just going to take the dogs for a walk; perhaps yo would like to join me?'

I was surprised to see that she had on one green and one black wellingt boot, both filthy dirty, and having seen better days.

h, help! I invited you to tea; not to go traipsing around the woods and sea
re with my smelly dogs – and you in your smart suit – but never mind, what
 feet do you have? Oh, as big as that, no matter, I'm sure we have a pair of
lies that would do; follow me and we'll see what the boot room can offer.'
ollowed her down numerous passages, past several suits of dusty armour, to
 boot room where she dug out an approximate pair of wellingtons, of almost
ilar colour and about the same size as each other, that I more-or-less fitted.
 these I tucked my business suit trousers, and having put my brief case in
 sitting room, and she having collected two large golden retrievers from in
it of the kitchen AGA, off we went.
e strode ahead at a fast pace, talking non-stop all the time about her dogs,
 son Kit, her sister Angela and the problems of being responsible for a
ely home that she didn't actually own; down through the overgrown
odland which, apart from some huge old oaks, consisted of very overgrown
dodendrons whose blossoms were now past their best. But I didn't have
 to stop and appreciate the scenery.
ome along, you *must* see the boat house and the boat, after all everybody
ts to see them, and I'm sure you're no exception, and let's face it, they've
 your company in a manner which it has enjoyed being accustomed to for
ast twenty-nine years.'
uldn't argue with that.
 made our way down the steep winding path, until, suddenly, we came to
each where the sea was lapping gently on the pebbly shore. There it was.
 famous boat house that held so many secrets and shadows of those fateful
 from the most famous of her novels. And there, further along the shore, at
dge of the woodland, was the little cabin cruiser which, in the novel, held
y more secrets of sudden death and sad memories.
ere. You've seen it. You can report back to your office that they really do
. Shall we make our way back, and find that tea I promised you. Then we
get down to business.'
 made our way back through the trees, which, with the sun now going down
ed rather dark and forbidding; and which, again brought memories of
 fateful days that she'd written of in that book, almost thirty years earlier.
made our way to the house where the housekeeper had laid out a tea of
ish delicacies and a pot of strong tea. We sat in the bay window
looking the large lawns. The setting sun, and the slate grey sea beyond
dling in my mind yet again, impressions of those events set out in fiction;
iver sneaked down my spine as I imagined that dour, sour-faced
ekeeper of the novel making such a misery of the life of the fictional
mbent of the house.
iness was quickly despatched and terms agreed, but she washed her hands
oletely of any personal appearances. Book signings, or any other literary
sions, were entirely out of the question.
 just not that type of person'

She hadn't left Cornwall for many years, and she didn't intend to start now. She wouldn't even consider a signing session at the local W.H.Smith's in Fow because, she said,

'It'll be a lot of W.I. ladies who'll be trying to get me either to join them, or g and talk to them about my life, and I've far more interesting things to do tha that!'

And so, as that first visit came to its end – a visit that was to mark the start a gentle and lasting personal friendship – I made my way back to my car wit thoughts still fresh in my mind, of Mrs Danvers, Rebecca and Manderley, o Menabilly, to give it its true name, with Daphne Du Maurier waving goodby from her ivy-covered porch in the shadow of the darkening trees around.

Then when the new book was finished, and selling well, I called again for te

I called again on many more occasions after that, and whenever it was t celebrate another new book, I would come away clutching a copy in which sl would have written a personal message.

3
Welcome Home

t was four-thirty on what had been a sunny and remarkably warm 3rd
January afternoon in 1964, when I drove into the driveway of the house we
red in Beckenham. Strange, I thought, the bedroom curtains were still
wn, surely the lazy devil wasn't still in bed?

)pened the front door and rushed back to the car to bring in my case; I'd
n away since Monday and couldn't wait to see him again; hoping everything
s all right. I'd worried about him so much while I was away.

vo doors faced me; one to the flat upstairs, the other to our ground floor flat.
re seemed to be a lot of post inside the porch way that separated the doors
he flats. On our door I noticed a small note attached with sticky tape.

*

ke many relationships, it started quite by chance. I had placed an
ertisement in the London Advertiser, 'Wanted. Single gentleman to share
bed flat, ideal for businessman, own bedroom share everything else,
10.0 per week incl. of rates and electricity. Split all other costs'. My previous
er, Gerald, a perpetual drunk, chain smoker and bed-wetter had had to go.
uld stand him no longer. Hence the advert.

as twenty-six, and still alone. If only I could find someone I could really get
vith, or hopefully something more. But someone to help pay the rent, and
round while I was away on business would be a start.

e advert brought a few enquiries but they were unsuitable. Two got to the
e of 'calling to view'. One was a wrestler who wanted a larger room than I
available, and wanted me to partner him when he practised!
e evening the 'phone rang. A well-spoken, young sounding voice with an
sual accent asked for further details about the accommodation. The caller
ned pleasant and educated, and I invited him to come and see for himself.
aid he would drop by the next afternoon 'before the evening performance'.
nge, I thought, perhaps I'm to have a budding star as a tenant. The next
rnoon the doorbell rang, and a young Indian man stood on the doorstep,
od afternoon, I hope I've come to the right address for the flat share.'
English was impeccable, but then, as I learnt later, he had been spent his
e school-life at Millfield Public School near Bath. I showed him around,
he joined me for a cup of tea.

modh Kumar's father was a steel manufacturer in Calcutta, but Pram
elf had spent his entire life in England under the guardianship of a
leman in the city.

Having discussed the rent and the probable other costs, my and his routine, the local transport and the trains to London, curiosity got the better of me. I couldn't wait to find out what Pram did for a living.

'Oh sorry, I should have said, I'm a dancer with the Royal Ballet.'

I was surprised, but only because I had never met a ballet dancer before, and had never been to the ballet.

We agreed terms, felt sure we could live together amicably, and decided that Pram would move in at the weekend. He 'phoned on the Friday to confirm his arrival the next day.

I slept fitfully Friday night, but couldn't understand why; I'd had other tenants, and in my job met strangers almost every day so what could be so different this time?

Eleven o'clock. The doorbell rang. There he was in a heavy white sweater and jeans looking like any other 1960s nineteen-year old. I showed him to his room and left him unpacking. At twelve-thirty I knocked at his door to ask if he fancied joining me at a nearby pub for lunch. He was dressed in white vest ballet tights and thick socks,

'I've been doing a bit of practicing before I go to 'the Garden' for formal practice before this evening's performance. I'm sorry I can't join you for lunch. I'll wait to eat until after the rehearsal when I'll have a snack with the rest of cast.'

'Don't be sorry,' I said, slightly disappointed, 'What are you dancing this evening?'

'Oh I'm just one of many peasants making a nuisance of himself with the village girls in *La Fille Mal Gardée*.' Although I had never seen that or any other ballet, I was very impressed and hoped that one day I'd see him on stage. He popped his head into the lounge as he was leaving and said he would see when he got back from 'the Garden'.

'Good luck, I hope it goes well.'

He hadn't returned by eleven-thirty, so I went to bed, leaving a note telling him to help himself to anything he wanted, and I'd see him in the morning.

The next morning, Sunday, I woke late as usual, and after pottering around the house doing the usual bachelor chores, I called Pram for breakfast. He'd helped himself to anything the previous night so I expected him to be hungry.

He emerged from his room in boxer shorts saying he'd have a quick shower and could he have just cereal and toast for breakfast?

'I thought you would be starving'.

'Starving I might be, but I must watch my figure if I am to dance.'

'Well you have a good figure for sure so I'll not encourage you to spoil it, but will you join me at a nice country pub I know for lunch?'

'Great, I'd like that. I'm not due back at the Garden until Tuesday so I can work it off by then.'

After breakfast he tidied his room while I collected the newspapers from shop along the road, and we sat in the lounge reading to a background

ditional jazz on the record player; already it was obvious that we had a lot in
nmon.

hope you're ok with the jazz?' he said, 'I find it relaxing after a night on stage
l constantly having to count the beats of music.'

was good to be relaxing in pleasant company.

certainly looks as though we shall to get on well together,' he said out of the
e, 'I just hope I don't do anything to spoil it.'

'hy on earth should you? You seem easy enough to get along with.'

es; - well I am usually, but I can get into some very dark moods at times,
ich lead me into some unattractive habits.'

decided not to go further along that path; at least not so early in our
ationship.

e drove to the Bickley Arms for a Sunday roast, and found a quiet table in a
ner.

ow before we order I want us to have this on me' said Pram.

hought we should go Dutch, as I'm sure a chorus dancer's pay can't be that
d.'

1, I don't rely on the money from the Royal; that's really just a hobby and
ough it's hard work, I enjoy it. No, I have a private income from my father,
ch is more than enough for my needs.'

s £600 a month from his father was a lot compared with my £150 plus a
Pram couldn't be bothered with a car, especially while living in London
1 plenty of public transport and enough money to pay for taxis when he felt
it.

x, I'll accept your offer this time but we mustn't make a habit of it or I'll feel
' I'm being kept,' I laughed.

vould quite like to keep you.'

s remark surprised me rather, so I brushed it aside. I was beginning to feel
Pram could be very good for me, and I had only known him for forty-eight
rs. Perhaps we could be good for each other?

en we got home I did some paperwork, and Pram went to his room to do
e practicing. Later we had tea and Pram said he was off to the local pub;
ld I join him? Not being a pub person I declined and said I would see him
:, or in the morning before I left for work. At that time I was a sales
esentative with McDougall's, the flour manufacturers.

im returned from the pub about eleven o'clock, a little the worse for drink,
ch saddened me rather as I had so recently got rid of Gerald because of his
king habits. I hope this new arrangement wasn't taking the same road.
n wasn't drunk, no where near it, but I could see it made him depressed
unhappy. Was this where his dark moods came from?

r lives jogged along like this for some weeks during which I frequently
zed him about the ballet, asking him to tell me the stories of the ballets,

and about the various dance steps, the costumes and what went on behind th
scenes.

'Tell you what, we've got a Royal Gala coming up soon and I'm allowed one
guest; would you like to come along and see for yourself? Perhaps you'll enjoy
perhaps you won't.'

'Do I have to dress up or will a suit do?'

'I know you have a dinner jacket, why not wear that, it'll be ideal because I
want you to come to the party after the performance, and I expect Princess
Margaret and Anthony Armstrong Jones will be there; but I warn you she can
get very loud and tends to swear a lot when she's had a few.'

I liked dressy occasions so I thought this would be a terrific idea,

The night of the Royal Gala arrived; dressed in the velvet-collared dinner
jacket, I'd recently bought from Austin Reed's I felt on top of the world as I
drove to Covent Garden. I took my seat in the stalls six rows back from the
orchestra pit, - wonderful. I looked behind me and up to the Royal Box that
would soon be occupied by members of the Royal Family. A fervent Royalist,
felt so proud.

A roll of drums from the orchestra pit; the entire audience stood, turned and
applauded as the Royal party entered their box. First the Queen Mother, then
Princess Margaret and Sir Anthony Armstrong Jones, her husband of about
twelve months, then the numerous ladies and gentlemen-in-waiting. I was ve
impressed. The orchestral struck up the National Anthem; our applause
followed, and we then sat to watch the performance.

My first visit to the ballet couldn't have been better. The enormous stage, th
beautiful music, the beautiful young dancers doing their best - it seemed - ju
for me. It moved me so much. I had no thought of anyone else around me. T
interval came, and I sat mesmerized by it all.

After the interval, Margot Fonteyn, Lyn Seymour, David Blair, Antoinett
Sibley, Merle Park and so many others, treated us to solos and *pas des deux*.
was spellbound by the clog dance from *La Fille Mal Gardée* and then a
ensemble in which Pram was included, and featured a morris-dance like
sequence with clashing sticks. I was so proud of him and he looked so
handsome.

At the performance end, the National Anthem was played again and w
remained standing until the Royal Party had gone.

Pram had told me to go to the stage door where he would meet me. What
melee! The entrance was packed with autograph seeking fans. They were to
unlucky as the stars were staying on for the after-show party.

I saw Pram forcing his way through the crowd towards me and I did the sa
towards him. Eventually he grabbed my hand and we made our way throug
the crowds into the back of the theatre. What a difference! Instead of plush
velvet seats, the gold decorations, and the crystal chandeliers there were bar
light bulbs, occasional fluorescent tubes, scratched paintwork and worn
linoleum. Pram hurried me through this maze of passages, ropes, pulleys an

ckdrops to the rear of the stage where a feast of cocktail snacks, bottles of ampagne, and numerous wines were laid out, with flunkies in their Covent rden outfits moving through the crowds, topping up drinks and offering bles. I was lost for words and could not stop looking around me, trying to e it all in. Eventually the curtains were opened, and there we were facing an pty theatre. I tried to imagine what it must be like being a dancer and facing t huge auditorium full of expectant and excited people. Pram dragged me und to meet some of his fellow chorus dancers; to some he introduced me as iend and to others as his landlord! Later the dancers were summoned to the nt of the stage, and stood in a large semi circle in readiness for Sir Frederick ton to introduce them to the Princess. I was so proud of Pram when he ved as he was introduced.

uring the party, Margot Fonteyn came across to Pram to congratulate him on performance along with the rest of the chorus, and I was flabbergasted en she turned to me, shook my hand, and said,

re you with the dance?'

o,' I replied, almost lost for words, 'I'm with McDougall's.'

h, how I wished a hole would open up and swallow me; I was so barrassed, but what else could I have said? But it didn't faze her,

h I'm sure that must be very interesting.'

didn't meet the Princess or her husband - but I heard her. I was not pressed. Her language was as bad as a train full of today's teenagers. I was cked; my respect for Royalty was to be severely dented from then on. I was glad that her mother had not accompanied her to the party.

was getting late. I suggested to Pram that we should quietly make our exit. wasn't keen on these after-show binges, and was thankful for my gestion. We made our way home in the car.

am was very quiet during the journey home, as we were nearing the house suddenly grabbed my hand.

m so glad you came this evening. I know you're not used to that sort of ction and you did so well - and I was so proud of having you there with me'. idn't know what to say, so I said nothing.

e arrived home, tired but contented, around 1.30am. Despite the hour, we entitled to a nightcap and having poured our drinks we settled down in our pective armchairs and discussed the evening. Then Pram moved across and on the floor between my legs with his back to me. His blue-black hair shone ne lamplight and, without thinking, I ran my fingers through it. I expected it e wiry but it was soft and smooth, I leant over and kissed it, it smelt of jas- e, which for some reason inexplicable brought tears to my eyes.

at's nice'.

s, I like doing it; do you know your hair smells of jasmine?'

o I didn't. Does that have some special significance for you'.

o I don't think so; I believe it's used by masseurs for giving sensuous ssages.'

'We must give it a try sometime.'

'If you would like it, we will.'

Soon his head fell forwards, and he was fast asleep. He being of slight build, was easily able to pick him up. I carried him to his bedroom, put him on the b and covered him with the quilt. He was still fast asleep. I wanted to lie beside him, but went to my own bed.

Shortly after, I heard my bedroom door open,

'Can't you sleep?'

There was no reply as he slipped into bed beside me.

'I hope you don't mind.'

I put my arms around him, and kissed him, and we made love.

We awoke to a sunny February Sunday morning; there was no embarrassme between us; I made tea and we drank it in bed, chatting as if nothing had happened between us. I made breakfast while Pram was in the shower, and w ate off trays in front of the sitting room fire; it was all so natural. Later that d after we had been for what had become our regular Sunday pub lunch, Pram moved his clothes and personal things into my room.

Our lives progress amicably for a couple of years; we were both content with the way things were working out, but I sensed it couldn't last; it was all too good to be true. I was now a devoted ballet fan and Pram got tickets for me whenever he could. At other times I would queue for tickets, a chore which often involved an all night vigil with a sleeping bag on the hard pavement outside the ticket office; but it was worth it.

Then one day, Pram came home and announced that he was giving up the ballet.

'I'll never be a star because I don't take it seriously enough,' he said, 'it's suc hard work and I'm paid a pittance which I don't need, whilst the Garden' asking the earth for tickets so that people can see us.'

He was silent for a moment, but I sensed his outburst wasn't finished.

'And I'm fed up of being classed as homosexual simply because all male dancers are expected to be queer. OK, even if I am, I don't want people talkir about me in that way.'

'So, what will you do? You can't just sit around doing nothing, especially wi your talents.'

'No, I won't sit around, I'd like to be a teacher; perhaps specializing in sport and PE.'

'That sounds a good idea, although I've no idea where you should start; I he you have.'

'Yes, I know what to do. I'll get something sorted soon.'

Within three weeks Pram had left Covent Garden, and then we both had t sleep out on the pavement for tickets because I refused to let him pay for me

A couple of months later he still hadn't done anything about his future and refused my offer to find out how to set about it. He spent more and more tin

the pub. I began to hate his coming home, but I loved him and wanted to
p him out of the rut he was getting into.
ate one night he returned home drunk, with a black eye and his clothes
odstained from a gash to his cheek.
What on earth happened?'
was protecting your reputation.'
What do you mean?'
Well, we've been seen out together every Sunday and people in the pub are
ing we're a couple of queers. Well I can't cope with it any more, I'm going to
back to girls in future and I'll move back into my own room.'
ou can't change your sexuality just like that,' I said, with a reasoning tone,
less, - perhaps, you're bisexual, which I can accept.' I hesitated slightly
ore continuing, 'but, even so, I wouldn't want you coming to my bed after
've been with a girl, and I don't think things can ever be quite the same with
n the future.'
o be it then! I'll stick to girls in the future, and I'll bring them back to my
m and shag them all night.'
knew it was only the drink talking and we would be back as we were
1orrow.
ut we weren't.
Ie drank even more, and brought girls back often, but hated himself
erwards and many times came crying to my bed in search of solace and love.
ved him the same as ever, but I knew this situation couldn't go on; he was
cing into slovenly habits, leaving me to change his sheets, wash his clothes
l clean his room.
ouldn't think how to help him when he wouldn't accept my help.

*

ook the note off the door, dreading what it might say. *Put out your cigarette
nce,* it said, I stubbed it out on the front step and opened the door, the smell
as was overpowering. I rushed to the meter under the stairs and turned it
it the stopcock. I ran to his room and found him lying neatly on his bed in
pyjamas, the room was a mess, with pills all over the floor and two whisky
les beside him, one empty, one still half full. The smell of gas, whisky and
th was overwhelming. I hurried to open the window and let the gas escape
uickly as possible; and to give myself some fresh air. I knew there was
ing I could do for my beautiful boy. I knelt beside his cold grey body,
king and kissing that blue-black hair, that still smelled of jasmine, and cried
heart out, blaming myself for not being stronger with him.

4
Our Twin Boys

They were not *our* boys;
    those two frightened boys at the foot of the stairs.
        The huge, dark oak stairs in the children's home.

They were not *our* boys;
    those two little boys
        who did not know their own names.
           'I'm Jon, and he's Alan.'
                'No I'm not; *I'm* Jon and he's Alan.'

They were not *our* boys;
    those two, shy little boys
        who didn't know what to do when taken to tea.
           'Do you like sugar?' we asked.
                'Do we?' they whispered to each other.

They were *becoming* our boys;
    those two little boys, who couldn't be taken to visit,
        so frightened they were that they'd be left behind - yet again.
Or, when called in for tea, hid their toys behind curtains,
    for fear they'd be stolen
        by some other child.

Whoopee! They *are* our boys now.
    In front of the judge in his dirty stained dressing gown.
        'Would you boys like to live with your new mum and dad
           - for as long as you want to?'
              'Yes please,' say *our* two little boys.

They *are,* now, our two little boys.

But, will *we* be good enough for them?

liff Probert

ginally from Tywyn, and, after leaving the Army aged twenty-one, Cliff urned to Barmouth to become a gift shop owner, a glass sculptor, and a ter. Several years later he opened Davy Jones's Locker, the now famous fee shop on Barmouth harbour. Further restaurateuring ventures included Penny Farthing Eating House, and then the Sangria restaurant – now a nese restaurant. He then decided to become a lobster fisherman, and nmissioned the first concrete boat in the area. Tiring of that, he took on a pidated Barmouth chip-shop, and turned it into the Mermaid – still a cessful business, under new ownership. Another change of direction took ce – but still in Barmouth – when Cliff and his wife took on, and renovated, Cors-y-Gedol Hotel which they subsequently sold on their retirement, after ing started the outdoor central market. Cliff now enjoys writing, has had first novel published, and has other books ready to be published.

lished book:
ritance Trafford Publishing (2007)
ISBN 142512077-6

5
The Novice

M ornin', Sir.'

, this is the Tinlin reach.'

w far? Oh, about three miles upstream from here.'

od fishing? Oh yes, the best there is on this stretch I'd say'

? Oh a long time, ever since I was a lad. My father was the ghillie in those s, so I learnt everything there is to know from him.'

I catch many salmon? Well I wouldn't be here if I didn't, would I? Only ng, Sir, but yes, I've caught a fair few in my time.'

you fish here? Of course I don't mind if you fish here. The river is open to yone, so long as they pay the licence fee.'

, you'll be all right there. Just set your things down by my old bag.'

'Seen better days? I'd say so. It were my father's, and he had it from his father but it's still got plenty of life in it yet.'

'Oh no. They don't make 'em like that any more, more's the pity.'

'You don't mind if I talk to you as you get ready, do you, Sir? You see, we don't get many experts fishing here nowadays, because of the cost. They can't afford it.'

'Me! Oh no, I don't have to pay, seeing as my father was the river bailiff for the Duke up at the castle.'

'You done much fishing before, Sir?'

'Your first time?'

'Well, you're in for a treat. Especially with all that new equipment you got there I'll wager you catch more fish then me, once you get set up.'

'Ah. Hold on a minute, Sir, I think I've got a bite.'

'Yes I have, and it's a big one too.'

'Hang on, Sir. Don't come too near, Sir while I play 'im in. How long? Oh, about ten minutes, so long as he doesn't get off the hook. Mmmmmm, there we are, my baby, come to daddy.'

'Yes you can help, Sir. Just bring that splendid new net of yours, and bring him gently out of the water, then up on to the bank.'

'What do I do now, Sir? I hit 'im on the head with this 'ere mallet. Oh no, he don't feel a thing, not if you're quick. Now, just let me take him out of the net.'

'It sure is a fine salmon, Sir.'

'How much does it weigh? Oh, about twelve pounds I should think.'

'What will I do with him? I'll take him up to the hotel and sell him, like I do all the others. That's how I get my beer money see.'

'Will *you* be able to catch one like this one, Sir? I'm sure you will. You can't miss with all that modern tackle you have there. Why don't you set it up and start fishing?'

'You're not sure how to do it, Sir? Haven't you fished before?'

ell, there's a thing. Never mind. I'll show you how to put it together. If that's
right with you, Sir?'

, I don't mind at all, Sir. Now, first we have to set up the rod. You just take it
 of the bag, and we'll see what you've got.'

 goodness! Never seen one like this before. What's it made of?'

rbon Fibre! Never heard of it. Still. If the shop where you bought it said it's
 best, who am I to say otherwise. You don't mind if I ask how much it cost,
you, Sir?'

ur hundred pounds! Well I never. My old dad only paid ten shillings for that
ient thing over there. Still, everything is expensive nowadays, isn't it, Sir?'

ght, now you've fitted the rod together, fix the reel between those two
ules on the handle.'

ich one? You mean you've got two reels? Goodness, I've only got one, and
t's about as old as Methuselah. But it still works, and I've caught many a fish
h it.'

ink you should put that one on. The other is for spinning, so you will need a
erent rod for that.'

. You've got one in the boot of the car? Well you only use that when the river
 flood, so it can stay there, unless you want me to show you how to use it?'

, go and get it if you like, while, I thread the line through these 'ere rings.'

, I don't mind, Sir. I can start fishing again when you're all set up.'

, that was quick, Sir!'

 You're anxious to begin fishing! Well, there's plenty of time. The fish won't
way. So, let's have a look at this other rod of yours. Yes, take it out of the
 Well, that looks a fine bit of equipment. May I hold it, Sir?'

 I don't think it is a bit stiff. It's supposed to be like that. It's made specially
pinning, you see. I expect it cost quite a lot, Sir. Like the fly rod there.'

at! Another two hundred? You don't do things by half, do you, Sir? Well,
r mind. Let's get you started.'

'What do you do now? You must choose a fly, and tie it to the end of the line.'

'Likely you'll find them in a tin box, in the basket.'

'Yes, that's the one. Now open it up, and let's see what you've got.'

'They certainly are very colourful, Sir, and very expensive too, I would think.'

'A hundred and fifty pounds!'

'The shop keeper said they were the best! I should think they were, at that price.'

'No. I don't think you were robbed, Sir. It's just that my old collection over there only cost a bob or two, 'cos I made them myself. Never mind, you choose one of yours and tie it on the end of the line.'

'Difficult! No, it's not difficult, Sir. Here, let me show you how to do it. There you are. Tight as your granny's arse. Oh sorry, Sir. I didn't mean to offend. It just a saying we have around here.'

'Well thank you, Sir, very noble of you.'

'Are you ready to start fishing now? Of course you are. But first, let me show you how to cast the line. We don't want you getting tangled in those trees behind us do we?'

'Right then. Just watch me as I hold my rod. See, nice and gentle, back and forth, like this, but don't go thrashing it about, or you'll scare the fish. So, let see if we can get a bite. Back and forth, back and forth, gently does it, *There*, that! Nearly had one then! Big 'un too. Are you watching?'

'You think you'd like to have a go now? All right. Come and stand by me. Take your rod in your right hand. Yes, like that. Now, hold the line in your left hand and take in the slack. That's it. Now bring the rod back over your head, and let the line sweep out behind you, like I did. Good. Now reverse the action and bring the line forward over the water. That's it! But don't be so fierce when you do it again. You're not supposed to thrash the hell out of the air like whip. Right, try again, but gently this time.'

'Keep going! Back and forth, like I showed you. Back and....Bloody hell! Be careful, you just missed my ear with the hook!'

. OK. Don't panic. It's all right, no damage done. It's all a matter of practice.
t keep trying and it'll come to you. Meantime, I think I'll just move a bit
her along the bank, and give you more room. You don't mind, do you, Sir.'

ank you, Sir, very kind of you I'm sure................ (*Silly bugger hasn't a clue.
's show him how it's done.'*)

m tee Tum tee Tum tee Tum, Catch a bugger by the bum. Mmmm, That's it,
y does it. There, got you my little beauty.'

at's that, Sir? Yes, I caught another one. How about you? Any luck?'

ll just keep trying, you'll get one in the end.'

re he comes. Into the net with you.'

, another beauty.'

velve pounder I should think. Like the first one!'

at's that! Why aren't you catching any? Maybe it's your equipment. You
w, new rod and everything. You have to nurse it. Treat it like a baby.'

w long could that take? Could be ages. Depends on the way it's made, and
you handle it. Take my rod for instance. It's built from spilt cane, not some
is new fangled carbon fibre stuff. You can't beat a good hand-made rod,
's what I always say.'

at was that, Sir? Is it because of the rod that you're not catching anything?
I don't know. It could be that it's not worn in yet.'

v long!'

t I couldn't say, Sir. I've not had any experience with carbon fibre, but I'd
illing to try.'

g on there, Sir. I've got another bite.'

Sir, another one, and it's a big blighter this time.'

Sir, You can help me land this beauty. Bring your net close, mine isn't
g enough. That's it. Gently does it. Blooming heck. Look at the size of it!
t be at least twenty pounds or I'm a Dutchman.'

'Will I be catching any more? No I don't think so. I'll just put these here fish my bag, and tidy up.'

'Yes, Sir, that's me done for today. I don't like to take too many out of the riv Must leave some for others, like yourself.'

'Of course you'll catch something, but I'm not sure you can do it with tha equipment. It's too new.'

'What's that, Sir? Would I sell my old rod? I couldn't do that, Sir. I'd not hav anything to fish with if I did, would I?'

'You mean, exchange your new rod for my old one?'

'Oh, I don't know. I'd have to think seriously about that.'

'What! You'd give me the spinner as well, and the reel!'

'No. I couldn't take the basket and the net. I'm quite happy with the ones I'v got. In any case, you'll need them when you come again, won't you?'

'You're not coming back again until next year, Sir! Why ever not?'

'You only came because of a wager! What wager would that be, Sir.'

'But you haven't caught any fish, have you?'

'Well, we can't have you lose the bet, can we, Sir. Tell you what. Seeing a you've been so generous, with the equipment and all, you take this twent pound whopper of a salmon with you, and when you get home, those partne in your office will have to eat their words, won't they.'

'That's all right, Sir. One favour deserves another, so they say. Well, I'll be o my way now. Thanks for the rods and the other things.'

'Yes, See you next year, maybe.....

..... *(or maybe not, hopefully.'*)

6

Border Crossing

The little family, huddled together, were terrified as they waited for night to fall. Desperate to escape the wrath of the Taliban, they had left their village er the cover of darkness, and now, hiding in this alien terrain, were tired hungry. Forced to flee when they heard that the tribal guerrillas were about ttack the peace force guarding their houses, they had had no alternative but ave quickly with only a little food, and the clothes on their backs.

shir had been an interpreter for the American forces, and would inevitably xecuted as a collaborator, so, together with his wife and two small children, left the village with the intention of reaching the Khyber pass and the safety akistan.

hat was two days ago, and after several harrowing moments, they had tually reached the foothills of the mountains. However, their ordeal was far over. With the sun beating down on the stones, the heat was unbearable, with their meagre supply of food and water gone, the children were erately hungry and thirsty. But there was nothing their parents could do hem. They dare not leave their hiding place among the rocks, having almost discovered earlier in the day. They must endure their discomfort until ness fell.

hen it did, they had the intense cold of another night to experience, and na, Bashir's wife, was terrified that her children, Tarig, and Kalila, would ze to death in their flimsy clothing. Tarig, a very intelligent boy of eleven, associated with the American soldiers, running errands for them. They had n him under their wing and introduced him to computers.

thin a few months he had become proficient with simple programmes, and ned the Internet in the search of knowledge. He learned a smattering of lish so that he could communicate with the men. If the Taliban had overed his ability, he too would have been in great danger.

e hurried journey through the arid landscape had sapped eight year old la's strength, and her father had been forced to carry her for most of the ney. It was vital that they move on as soon as it was dark, but it would be cult if they did not find water soon.

er three hours of torment, the sun disappeared behind the mountains, and ground began to cool. Their respite was brief. The night sky began to en, bringing the intense cold with it.

shir grieved for his family, and knelt on the hard ground, praying to Allah eliverance. Miraculously, after only a few minutes, it seemed his prayers t be answered. High above, the jagged peaks of the mountains were lit up ghtening. In minutes a violent thunderstorm raged, and the water they so erately needed streamed down ravines and crevices. For a moment the

family were safe from danger, and they hastily filled their plastic bottles. The
they had to move quickly; there was the likelihood that floods would destroy
the trail they were to take into the high mountains. Baked by the unrelenting
sun, then soaked by the freezing rain, the chupan of father and son, the chan
of the woman, and the thin dress of her daughter, clung to them like second
skins. But they must move on, or face hyperthermia and possible death.

Bashir gathered his little family together. They must trust in God and make
their bid for freedom. Little Kalila, reluctant to leave her arms, clung tightly
her mother's thin body. Tarig though was stronger and ready to continue
Though he was cold, their trek was an adventure, and he looked forward to
leaving Afghanistan and going to America; America, the wonderful place he
seen on the Internet.

Bashir and his family, fearing what lay ahead, started out on what they hop
would be the final day of their ordeal. It was not easy for them. In the darkne
the steep path was difficult to see because mud and water obliterated much o
the trail. The rock strewn ground was treacherous, often causing them to fall
but they struggled on until they found the main track which led up to th
border post.

This trail, the main artery between Pakistan and Afghanistan, was the rout
by which merchandise and illegal armaments passed between the two
countries. Heavily laden horses and donkeys carried their loads to the town
and villages far below.

The hazardous journey, fraught with danger from brigands and thieves, wa
long and exhausting. Despite their fear, traders stopped to prepare meals.

With his family near starvation, Bashir approached a group of men who we
cooking their meal over a fire, and asked if he could buy a little food. He hel
out his hand, offering what little money he had, hoping the traders would se
their plight and feel sorry for the children.

'Where are you from?' grunted one of the men, beckoning the children t
come closer to the fire. He placed his arm round the girl.

'Why are you dragging these children through the pass, they look as if the
haven't eaten for days?'

Bashir was in a quandary, if these men were Taliban he was in seriou
trouble. Pre-empting his father, Tarig, in his wisdom replied,

'My grandmother is very sick, but we are trying to get to Karachi, so tha
Mama can look after her.

'Is this true?' the traveller asked the girl, and she, in her innocence, shook
head.

'Hm, I thought so.'

He looked gravely at the pathetic little group, then muttered to his
companions. Bashir was petrified. He realised their fates lay in the hands o
these three individuals. Without another word, the trader reached into th
cooking pot and heaped a mound of rice onto a tin plate, over which he ladl
some curry sauce.

Iere.' He said, holding out the plate.

The family gratefully accepted the offering, and huddled together on the und, balled the rice in their fingers and ate their first food in more than two 's.

ashir took little of the rice. Whilst his family ate, he moved over to thank the n for their generosity. From their conversation it was revealed that they too e against the Taliban ideology; and wished Bashir and his family a safe sage through the border post. But this last comment made Bashir aware that ir troubles were not ended. In their panic to leave his village, he had gotten about documents, and without them they would not be allowed to s through the border control. He was devastated by the realisation of his pidity. After all their hardship, they would have to retrace their steps and arn home. With death assuredly awaiting him if the Taliban had taken over village, he would rather die here on the mountain, than go back. But he had family to think of. Hopefully, if he gave himself up, his wife and children ht be safe from the wrath of the Mujahdin.

e gathered his family together and turned to face the way back down the l, but before he had taken a step, one of the traders asked where he was g. Bashir explained their predicament. Urging them to wait, the men went a huddle. The leader then walked to one of the horses, and produced a dful of documents from a pannier. He handed them to Bashir.

ere, take these, they should get you safely across the border. If you have any culty, just tell them what your son told us. That you are going to nurse your her-in-law, who is dying. Be subservient, and brief with your answers. Use children to soften up the patrol; they have a soft spot for juveniles.'

ashir was overwhelmed. How could he thank them? Should he offer them r last few afghanis?

was astounded at what happened next. One of the other men passed him a ch containing some rupee's, as another handed him a small bag of rice. air fell to his knees with gratitude. But the leader reached forward and raced him.

is nothing my friend, I have a family of my own, and understand your eration. Now we must be on our way, we have friends expecting us in ul.'

thout waiting for a reply, he and his comrades turned their backs, leading r pack animals down the trail.

ving thanks to Allah and with food and money to see them on their way, r and his family started out on the last leg of their journey.

ook them the rest of the day to reach the high pass. With the border post st in sight, Bashir prayed their entry into Pakistan would be trouble free. vas trembling with the sweat of fear as they finally approached the frontier. heavily armed sentry motioned them to stand in the queue of travellers ing to enter the custom house.

Slowly the column moved forward until there were only a dozen people in front of Bashir. Hardly able to control his panic, he held the documents in his hand. His fears were heightened when a man, protesting his innocence was hustled out of the office and brutally beaten by the roadside. There was a feeling of unease, and low muttering by the people waiting in the line.

The man in front of Bashir turned to him,

'I told him not to show false papers, but he wouldn't listen.'

Having seen the consequences should their papers be found to be forged Bashir was in a mind to turn back. But his wife laid her hand on his arm.

'You are too nervous. Give me the papers. When we get inside, let me speak the authorities; and Tarig, if they ask you questions, whatever happens, you must tell the truth, do you understand?'

Her son nodded his head in compliance.

It was time.

A guard came out of the building.

'Next!'

He ushered the family into the room. An intimidating thick-necked officer wearing an army uniform, sat behind a desk. Bashir stood in fear and trembling.

'Your papers,' the man barked aggressively, holding out his hand. He raised his eyebrows when it was the woman who reached forward and produced the papers. After having scrutinised them briefly, he looked up.

'Why do you want to come to Pakistan?' he asked brusquely.

Bashir was about to speak when Sabina laid her hand on his arm. She turned to the officer.

'I was always taught not to lie, and I cannot lie to you now. We are fleeing from the Taliban. My husband is an interpreter for the American army. If we are forced to return to our village, he will be killed. It is as simple as that.'

There was a frosty silence in the room. The officer waived the papers before them.

'You know these are false, don't you?'

Sabina nodded, the tears streaming down her cheeks.

'Then I must have you imprisoned and sent back to where you came from.' leaned forward menacingly. 'Now, empty your bags quickly. Take everything out of your pockets, and put them here on the desk.'

Reaching out, he ran his hands through their few pathetic belongings Rummaging through Tarig's meagre possessions, he opened his exercise book and a picture of the Statue of Liberty fell out. He pounced on it quickly.

'Where did you get this?' he demanded harshly.

'The Americans in our village gave it to me, sir,' Tarig stuttered. 'I saw the picture when I was using their computer. I wanted one like it because it looked like a guardian angel, so they printed one out for me. Did I do a bad thing, sir

The officer's face relaxed for a brief moment. Impressed by the boy's frankness, he leaned back in his chair,

Vell, maybe, maybe not. The Americans are not very popular in our country,
 advise you not to show this to anyone. Do you understand?'
arig flinched, trying to hold back his tears. There was a long pause as the
cer looked long and hard at the bedraggled family.
'ou realise that by presenting false papers, you have forfeited the right to
er my country, don't you?'
nowing his children would have to endure the tyranny they had left behind
m. Bashir bowed his head and nodded. His dream of freedom was over.
ne officer leaned forward and pushed their belongings towards them.
uickly, take them away.'
he family scrabbled their things together and waited for his sentence, but
elievably the officer pointed to the door,
ow GO, GO and don't ever return!'
t had happened. They were free. Their weariness left them as they
fidently headed forward towards Pakistan, and maybe, one day, to America,
Statue of Liberty and freedom.

7

The First, but not the Last

A foot most carefully and delicately poised,
encased and swathed in layer on
layer of protective plastic lumber,
lowers slowly, feather like, until first contact
with the unfamiliar mass gives reassurance
of solidity beneath the explorative member.

A pause, then the partner of this foot,
now reassured, descends with positive action
and joins the other on the aluminium ladder,
to thrill to this first incredible experience.

The decision to make, and take, their first faltering
but measured treads, with touch so light, almost
defying gravity, elates and overwhelms the walkers,
until reality grips with the realisation that this
unfamiliar place has now become just another
conquest to be placed in history,
taken as commonplace,
while each new discovery
bounds along to cover over the other, as the dust
now gently settling, obscures the first footprints
on this now familiar lunar landscape.

8
Artistic Licence

tanding with palette in one hand, and brush in the other, I surveyed the still
life items I'd arranged on the table. My montage of a tin of baked beans, a
s of cherry tomatoes, and a clove of garlic may seem an odd group of things
aint, but, until my wife came back with the weekend shopping, these were
only things I could find in the kitchen. With the anticipation of a hassle free
ning, I was poised to dip my brush into the yellow ochre, when the 'phone
. Quietly and calmly, I laid down the brush.

ello'

I could hear was a rumbling sound in the background.

ello,' I said again, somewhat agitated, as my creativity was quickly being
ked.

as about to repeat the question when a strident voice in my ear shouted,
be there in ten minutes! Tell Margaret!'

fore I had a chance to answer, my mother-in-law cut me off. 'Bloody hell.
's all I need at this moment.'

ieving myself of the phone and the palette, I hurried to the sitting room to
e sure everything was tidy, and in good order.

u see, Gladys, my mother-in-law, is a fastidiously arrogant woman, and I
well aware of the tirade which would follow if she found anything not up to
standard. Albeit she was the daughter of a rag-and-bone man, who had
his trade with a horse and cart.

ad just about finished, when I heard her car coming up the drive.

mmit, she's here already!

tting on a brave face, I stepped into the hall, and opened the front door.
ar had come to a stop, and there she was, with her bottom sticking out
behind the driver's door, rummaging, for what I presumed would be her
ninous handbag.

aited with trepidation as she extricated herself, and marched purposefully
rds me, and the front door.

here's Margaret?' She demanded as she brushed me aside and entered the
e. 'I have something important to tell her.' Margaret is my wife.

hout waiting for a reply, she took off her coat and hung it with the others
e hall. Then, still totally ignoring me, she turned towards the stairs.

argaret, where are you, dear? I need to see you urgently!'

e's not here. She's gone to see Susan, and do some shopping. She won't be
until this afternoon.'

dys turned and faced me with her evil eyes.

d what am I supposed to do until then? You know I must have food before
clock, or my ulcer will play havoc with my intestines.'

'Good luck to them,' I thought to myself, 'they'd have a battle on their hand they thought they could get the better of this old dragon. But, I must be civi After all, she is a guest in my home – more's the pity.'

'Don't worry, mother-in-law,' I said cheerfully. 'How about I rustle someth up for your lunch, then you can wait in the sitting room until Margaret come back.'

'I don't suppose I have any alternative, do I? But I can't wait all that long. must have something to drink, or my poor body will shrink to nothing.'

'And the sooner the better,' I thought spitefully, as I ushered her into th kitchen, and seated her at the table.

'What would you like,' I asked, as I filled the kettle, 'tea, or coffee?'

'It isn't instant coffee, is it?'

'I'm afraid it is, until Margaret returns with the shopping.'

'You know very well I only drink fresh coffee. I can't abide that cheap freez dried stuff. I'll have tea!'

That was an order, and I'd better get on with it. There were two mugs on th draining board, and I was about to drop a tea bag in each, when she let out tongue-lashing rebuke.

'I can't drink out of a mug! I must have a china cup and saucer! And I don want one of those disgusting tea bags either; they're full of dust and sweepir from the floor. Don't you have any fresh Earl Grey?'

'I'll Earl Grey you in a minute.' I thought furiously, but I knew we had som leaf tea in the cupboard, and reached up for it.

'Two spoonfuls, and one for the pot,' she said before I had even opened tl tin, 'and don't forget to warm the pot!'

'I had a good mind to warm her with the boiling kettle; but thought better it. I'd only have to attend her funeral if I did.

Reaching into the cupboard, I took out a best cup and saucer. When the te was infused to her satisfaction and I was about to pour she berated me one again.

'Put the milk in first. You'll spoil the flavour.'

I held my breath and poured the milk. Before I could lift the teapot she sa must use a tea strainer.

'Don't you know anything about making tea, Cyril? If you don't use a strai the cup will be full of bits. You should know that!'

Thankfully, I found a strainer in the drawer, and poured the tea.

'Is that to your satisfaction, Gladys?' I asked, subserviently, as I placed tl cup and saucer before her.

'Don't be facetious, Cyril,' she said, and with her little finger extended, sl lifted the cup to her lips. But disaster struck. The cup slipped, fell from h hand, and dropped to the kitchen floor, breaking into several pieces. To ma matters worse, the tea had splattered her dress. For a second she was speechless. It was wonderful, but short-lived. She gave a gasp of fury, lurch feet, and walked unsteadily into the sitting room, where she plonked herself n among the cushions on the sofa.

think I'm going to faint,' she muttered feebly, but then recovered instantly, all your fault. You made the tea too hot.'

K. OK. it's all my fault,' I thought wearily as I handed her a towel.

y yourself with this, then sit back peacefully and watch the television while ke some lunch.' I handed her the remote control.

t's not working properly!' she said, petulantly, jabbing it towards the ision set and pressing every button. I took it from her, and adjusted it to ive BBC 1. The antiques programmes were about to start.

ll that do?'

s, it's what I always watch at home.' She turned her head, asked what she having for lunch, but didn't wait for a reply, which was handy as I hadn't slightest idea what to give her.

as in a quandary. There would be no food until Margaret came home with shopping. All I had were the baked beans, the tomatoes, and the garlic – my life collection in the studio. I knew she would balk at the thought of baked s, let alone garlic. She might just tolerate the tomatoes, but that was all. I had an inspiration, and having always fancied myself as an adventurous , decided to cobble up a meal with just those three ingredients. I would e the old hag a veggie meatloaf.

th baked beans tipped into the blender, four of the six tomatoes popped on and then the garlic – ready steady go! But as I switched on the blender, the e of its motor brought mother-in-law out of her trance. She came charging the kitchen.

rn that thing off! You've ruined the picture on the television! I was just ing for the expert's valuation of a china vase when the interference from blasted thing ruined the conversation. Now I'll never know how much my piece is worth.' And having dropped that little gem, she stormed out.

t why should I worry, I'd almost finished my recipe preparations – until, is, I stuck my finger into the mixture to have a taste. It was too runny - how I thicken it? I remembered the sandwich Margaret had left me for lunch. k slice of ham between two thick slices of wholemeal bread – that should e trick. Out of the fridge, carefully cut one slice of bread into triangles for ide plate, and the rest into the blender. Switch on again, and await Gladys's h. But she failed to appear.

d, has she died?' I hoped vengefully. No such luck. She was fast asleep in itting room. And yes, I admit, I was rather deflated.

th the mixture out of the blender and into a loaf tin, and the meatloaf into ven, I now needed to hunt down some salad leaves. In the garden I found a le of mangy lettuces that had not quite bolted, and which were only half by slugs. Judicious stripping of outer leaves, and we were OK. I had k gold. Now it was time to show off my artistic abilities away from the .

Gladys slept on.

Meatloaf now out of the oven, and undergoing an emergency cooling of period in the deep freeze. Best linen place-mat on the dining room table with best knife and fork! There was no way she was going to complain about our cutlery or china. Now, with a best breakfast and side plate out of the cabinet was almost there. Everything had to be best.

And Gladys still slept on. God was on my side.

Meatloaf from the freezer. Would it turn out in one piece, or slither out like wet blancmange? Thank you God. It was perfect. But before I presented it to her majesty, I must first taste it. In the event that it was disgusting, I had decided beforehand that I would let the dragon sleep until Margaret came home.

So. here goes. Shit or bust,' I thought as I cut a sliver and placed it on my tongue. It was perfect – even if I do say so myself. There was no way that my dear mother-in-law could say otherwise. Now to assemble my masterpiece. Spotlessly clean plate, three slices of meatloaf neatly in the centre, two crisp lettuce leaves on one side, and two vine tomatoes – carefully halved, so that when she cut them they would not burst and splatter their seeds over her dr

It was done. I took the dish into the dining room and placed it beside the f triangles of wholemeal bread lying on the side plate.

Time for Armageddon! I entered the sitting room and found the dear lady sleeping like a baby. I resisted the temptation to shake the hell out of her, but gently prodded her shoulder. She jumped up with a start.

'Huh!' she stuttered, spittle slithering down her chin, 'Where am I!'

She gazed up at me with bleary, uncomprehending eyes.

'Who are you?' she blurted out in panic.

I felt like slapping some sense into her, but fought hard against the attract of such action.

'It's me, Gladys. Cyril. Your son-in-law. Your tea is ready.'

At the mention of food, she came round quickly.

'About time too!' she muttered crustily, as she struggled to get up from the sofa. I leaned forward to help her, but she thrust my hand away.

'No need to touch me. I don't need your help!'

'Please yourself, you old bitch,' I thought as she walked ditheringly into the dining room.

Before sitting down she leaned forward, and inspected her plate of foo Luckily it seemed to pass muster, and she sat heavily in the chair. She prod the loaf with her fork, the sniffed it.

'What is it? I hope it's not meat. You know I'm a vegetarian.'

I assured her it contained no meat.

She cut a small portion, and lifted it to her mouth. I waited with bated bre for the explosion of revulsion which I was sure to follow. To my surprise, sh tucked in, and ate everything on the plate. Standing behind her, I punched

with elation. I had fooled the old biddy! Little did she realise she was eating
ed beans, ham and an entire bulb of garlic.

hat was very nice,' she said, wiping her mouth on the serviette. 'I must ask
rgaret for the recipe.'

that moment my wife walked through the door.

ello Mother!' she said with surprise as she dropped the groceries on the
r. 'How long have you been here? Why didn't you tell me you were coming?
ouldn't have gone shopping if you had let me know. Did you want
ething? Have you eaten?'

's okay Margaret,' I said cheerfully, 'Your mother is fine; aren't you Gladys?'
Gladys was a little confused by all her daughter's questions, and only
aged to nod.

ut has she had anything to eat, Cyril? You know she has to eat regularly.'

s all right, Margaret. I had some of that lovely vegetarian loaf you made. I
quite full now. You must give me the recipe so I can pass it on to my
ds.'

argaret's bewilderment was plain to see, but I placed my finger to my lips,
she did not pursue the matter.

aving mother and daughter to themselves I sneaked back into my studio.
ed on my stool, I contemplated the empty table. Who would have thought
, even though I had been prevented from painting them, a tin of baked
is, a few tomatoes, and some garlic could have given me so much pleasure
eative and otherwise.

9
Lord of the Dance

'**Y**ou are cordially invited to the ball at Buckingham Palace'

The invitation dropped through my letter box. Luckily I had a dress suit. looked forward to the event with great anticipation.

I was overwhelmed as I entered the ballroom. Not only by the opulence, bu the guests assembled. The Royal Family, together with lords and ladies, an men of distinction were in attendance. Had I made a terrible mistake? Presenting my invitation, the flunky crossed my name off the list, and I wa ushered forward.

Flipping heck, what do I do now? The orchestra started to play and couple took to the floor.

Trying to look inconspicuous as I sidled round the perimeter of the ballroo was dying to ask someone to dance – but it was impossible.

But then I thought 'dammit, why shouldn't I request a dance?' I pushe through the crowd, and found myself standing next to the Queen and Princ Phillip. She tapped her feet in time to the music, and without thinking I aske I might have the next waltz. She paused momentarily, then smiled and stoo up. I took her hand and we stepped down to the dance floor.

When the dance ended, I escorted her back to her seat. She gave a smile, th requesting a sword from the nearest dignitary, asked me to kneel.

It was then I woke up!

aggi West

*ggi, linguist extraordinaire, born and educated in Northern Ireland, now
s in Harlech and her entire life has been embroiled in words. She loves
ds in every guise, and, we are told, even reads corn flakes packets and yo-
rt pots in her quest to assuage her word-fascination. And she's the same
h numbers too. Much of Maggi's life was spent in London, where – not sur-
singly – she worked in a bookshop. Maggi has four children, including a
ghter in America, and several grandchildren, and two great-grandchil-
n. She is a keen chorister, and her interests include words, trees, ayurvedic
plimentary medicine, herbs, gardens, and geology. Maggi was a member
n over 60s drama group which won first place at a festival in Ireland in
6. A born story-teller, Maggi has the gift of the most eloquent and delight-
jab, often holding us in spellbound silence. She is an information junkie,
has an enormous store of jokes.*

10
Learner's Lament

There's something that I want to do,
It's learn to speak Welsh, just like you,
But I had not the least idea
Of the pitfalls I might learn to fear.

Used to the masculine being he,
In Wales I find that *hi* means she,
Both pronounced the same of course.
No wonder I end up off course.

Feminine adjectives have mostly gone,
But please remember *'y ford gron'*.
Cats or chairs, two three or four
Number is feminine, as before.
Nouns come first, adjectives after,
But some are in front – please, no laughter!

English use 'more' to compare,
In Welsh *mor lân* means fair.
And all those different words for 'yes'
Make life difficult I'll confess,
But not as bad as the language of the Eskimo
Where there are a hundred words for 'snow'.

Then there are those Welsh sounds
Which give us so much trouble.
When we try to say *ll*
We end up blowing bubbles!
There's *ch* and *dd* and *ff* and *ng*
All well articulated.
It really is no wonder
That our efforts all seem fated.

Another source of trouble:
Ubiquitous Welsh mutations;
I've thought about appealing
To the United Nations!
You try to look a word up
And find it's not in the book,
Then you realise it's mutated
And, at last, you're off the hook.

It's such a charming language,
With words like *'popty ping'*
And many words we ought to know
Because of borrowing.
But it really is confusing,
And it gave me quite a shock,
When at last I realised
That every *ffrog*'s a frock!

And what about all those women,
Nessi, Pam and Beth?
I've tried to get them into my head
Will I manage before I'm dead?

In spite of all this hassle,
I intend to persevere.
When will I be fluent?
Not for many a year!

11

Surprise in Store

he wandered through the house rather disconsolately, feeling vaguely uneasy. The children were at school, and it was not her cleaning lady's day.
thought about her friends, and one-by-one she ticked them off in her mind
course, it was Thursday, she'd forgotten, they were all busy on Thursdays.
wondered why she felt so restless. Perhaps she should think about
rning to work. She didn't really have enough to occupy her now.
e went into her airy bedroom and gazed at herself in the long mirror. She
dn't help feeling a little smug. She'd kept her figure and her skin had always
n good, and she didn't yet have any grey in her hair. Then she had an idea.
would go up to town and surprise George. She might even treat him to
h. She would go by train; parking was so difficult now with all these meters
things, and there had probably been some changes in the traffic flow that
was no longer familiar with. She changed her clothes and put a few
ntials into a good leather handbag, and left the house, careful to set the
m as she did so.
e drive to the station was uneventful, and the station had plenty of room in
car park so she had no trouble parking. She bought a magazine and her
t, and waited for the train. She had judged it well; it came along in only a
minutes. Having found a seat without difficulty, she flipped through the
azine; it really didn't have anything interesting this month, and she
dered why she had bothered. Magazines were really all the same. They all
you what you should do to keep young and beautiful, feed your family well,
the sparkle in your marriage and organise your home. She could probably
e one all by herself.
e watched as the countryside slipped by; houses, schools, tiny country
ches surrounded by their tiny graveyards. In a way she envied the people
lived and died in those little villages. They probably had a better life than
ad, she thought. There would be a greater sense of community than in her
hbourhood with the upmarket houses and manicured lawns.
e thought about her friends. She called them friends, but they weren't
y. True they had some things in common; children, nice houses, husbands
g well in the city. But what did she really know about them? She thought
t her mother who had had a struggle to bring up her family. She realised
she was doing, and pulled herself up sharply. She had been very lucky.
ge was a good husband, a fond father. They wanted for nothing.
e train slowed, then stopped. She suppressed a little sigh of impatience.
remembered the crash at Paddington and was glad they were being
ous. Why was she upset by the delay? George didn't know she was coming.

The train was late getting in. She decided not to 'phone George, but to go instead to her favourite department store and browse. There was no hurry; it wasn't her week for the school run. She had a light snack in the café, and began to wander. Nothing caught her eye in the fashion department so she gravitated, as always, to the lingerie.

As she approached, she saw a familiar figure. It was George. It wasn't her birthday, or anniversary; he didn't have a sister, and anyway if he had he wouldn't buy her gorgeous silk underwear like the pile of things the assistant was handling so reverently. They couldn't be for her because she loathed red and had often told him so, and even George was not that absent-minded.

'Hello, George.' she said.

12
Prose Poem

A t last she reached the glade.
    She squeezed though the hole in the ugly fence
      they had erected
        She had been there so often with her father.

She looked around, and drank it all in.
    The haze of blue beneath the beeches
      interspersed with white and pinky flowers.
      The sunlight revealed the tiny silver hairs
        on the tender young beech leaves.

She closed her eyes and concentrated on the sounds:
    the birds, the insects, the little stream.

She had lived this moment so often.

Opening her eyes, she saw at her feet,
    quivering, a trapped butterfly.
      Gently she moved the tiny twig which held it prisoner.
      It fluttered feebly, then stopped.
        Her heart fluttered too.
        It moved again.
          She sighed with relief.
Somehow she felt her destiny was inextricably
    bound up with this tiny creature.

What would happen when she saw the specialist tomorrow?

13
The Find

was a lovely Spring day. The sky was blue and everything in the garden
seemed to be bursting into growth. I was trying to get ahead with the
sework because it was my birthday and I was being taken to the theatre to
brate. The children were not yet old enough to be left on their own, so I
ted to get the house tidied up so the baby-sitter would not turn tail and run.
vas hoovering in the sitting room when two of the children came bursting
t was the first day of the Easter holidays.

lum, Mum, come quickly. Come and see what we've found. There's a big
bag in the drive and it's got lots of things in it!'
he Drive' was the way up to a big house close by. The children used to go
ugh a hole in the fence and play among the trees.

t first I thought they might be playing a joke on me, but they were very
stent so I switched off the hoover and went with them. They took me down
garden, helped me through the hole in the fence and showed me. There,
ing up against a tree, was a blue laundry bag. It was full of things made of
er. I knew one should not move things as a rule, but I reckoned that
eone had stolen them and stashed them there, intending to collect them
r. I thought the best thing to do was to take the bag into the house and
ne the police. The bag was heavy, but between us we managed to get it
ugh the fence and into the house.

nce there, I opened the bag and looked at the contents. It was a real find.
re was a cigarette box, entrée dishes, photos in silver frames, a tray, two
uettes in silver frames and a packet of chops from Tesco.

I looked at the silhouettes, I couldn't help thinking, *'they'd look nice up
e on the wall'*. I didn't let the children handle things because of finger
ts and I was very careful myself.

nesty won, and I rang the police. That was the start. Shortly after, a police
rrived, then another. Each new arrival had to be shown where the bag had
found. It was rather funny, seeing these usually tidy men after they had
e been through the hole in our fence. The children felt very important.
rally they were very excited too.

en the police asked '..and how did you come to find the bag?' they were
clear.

um said we could go out 'cos it was a nice day and we decided to go to the
ollow tree, didn't we John?'
s, and we saw the bag when we went through the hole in the fence and we
over then looked inside. We thought we'd better tell you Mum'.

'Are you going to take our fingerprints? Mum says you can tell people by th
fingerprints. She says everybody has different fingerprints. She said you mig
take ours 'cos we might have touched something. Are you going to?'

'We can't do it now, but maybe you could come to the station. We could do
there'.

The police took the bag away. They told us that the things had been stolen
from a house in a neighbourhood close by, just a few hours earlier. Apparent
the owner had reported the theft not long before we rang the police.

The next day, a great big bouquet of all sorts of spring flowers was delivere
to the house. It was beautiful, but we didn't really enjoy them because we we
away for Easter, and when we came back they were dead.

The children never did have their fingerprints taken. They were disappoint
about that.

14
Jumper

It's a very odd place to end up in.
I ain't seen aught quite like this.
If I 'adn't been warned all abaht 'em
I'd fink someone was takin' the piss.

Only two legs, that I can see,
My other 'omes 'ad four.
And as I look arrahnd me,
I fink I see some more.

Why are they all so different?
What are they all so bare?
They ain't got fur all over,
They only 'ave some 'air.

And they all move so slow,
They seem to take forever.
And yet I'm sure that I've been told
They're really very clever.

I believe that they're called 'umans,
And if I'm not mistaken,
They eat lots of different things,
Like vegetables and bacon.

I wonder if they all taste the same,
I wonder 'ow they feel,
I fink I'll try anuvver one,
It's time for my next meal.

15
Public Servant

A public servant, it's my vocation
To take what's not wanted
And get rid of it for the nation.

I'm often looked for anxiously
And found with great relief,
Some sit down gratefully and sigh
I wonder why.

I never refuse them entrance.
They visit me every day
But what of their behaviour?
How do they repay...

...me for the relief I give?
I just don't think it's right
That when they don't like something
They call it ....

When they need to come and see me
They often have a pain.
Each day
I take what they don't want
They treat me with disdain.

Sometimes they don't make it
Then what is my reward?
A nasty mess upon the floor
And graffiti on my door.

They often pinch my paper,
But what really makes me blush,
Is when they use me carelessly
And don't even flush.

16
Unexpected Treasure

'**G**ood Morning,' called Liz cheerfully as she entered the shop one Monda
morning, 'Have you had a good weekend?'

She got the usual replies.

'Not too bad.'

'So So.'

'*I wonder if anyone will ever say 'yes.'* she thought as she went down th
stairs to the basement. Curious how few people ever answer questions
positively.

She enjoyed her job running a charity shop for *Age Concern*. It was full o
variety; you never knew what a day would bring.

She opened the door to her office-cum-storeroom and gasped. Forty blac
plastic bags full of donations took up most of the available floor space. It wa
obvious that a lot of reorganisation would be needed. She often had a lot to c
with on a Monday if she had had a Saturday off. When old people died thei
relatives often had to clear their things over the weekend. In this poor
neighbourhood they could not afford to take off more time that was absolute
necessary.

She made some space near the long table so that things could be examine
and sorted as easily as possible. She got a fresh supply of black bags so tha
items not good enough to sell could be put in straight-away for recycling. As
worked her mind wandered. She had heard on Friday that old Mrs Meredit
had died. She was sorry. Mrs Meredith had been one of her favourite
customers. Although not in the best of health she always seemed to be cheer
So many old people were miserable but Mrs M was one of the 'happy few'. S
had not had an easy life. She had lived all her life in the East End and kne
what it was to have to go without. She had been a child in the Second Worl
War and had been 'blitzed out' several times. Her father had been killed in t
war and her older brother severely wounded, and yet one of he favourite sor
had been *Stick a geranium in yer 'at and be 'appy.* She would be missed. Sh
had married and had four children, two of whom lived abroad now, but he
youngest daughter lived quite close by and had been able to keep an eye on
mother, who was fiercely independent.

She worked methodically; it came of long practice. Open bags carefully, yo
never know what might be inside. There had been several near accidents wh
objects wrapped in clothes had been broken in transit and volunteers had b
scratched, in not actually cut.

'Lucky we had a sale last week,' she thought. 'Always have to have a sale in
spring to clear our as many bulky winter things as we can.' Prices in the sho
were low, but when they were even lower, people still examined things

efully. There were many one parent families, and money was tight at the
t of time. They could not afford to waste it.

 she worked she was quite often interrupted. It was a shop policy never to
 anything which had lost its price tag. Liz was the ultimate authority.
netimes tags came adrift if the price gun was playing up, but sometimes
tomers would remove them in the hope that they would get the item even
aper. She remembered the last time this had happened, and couldn't help
ling to herself. It had been only a couple of weeks before. She had taken up
eral jackets, and hung them up. Ten minutes later she was called; one of the
kets had no tag. The woman who wanted to buy it was well known to the
f. She always managed to find things without prices. Remembering the price
 had put on it Liz added a pound. The woman paid up.
rve her right' Liz thought.

me for a break. Liz went upstairs to have coffee with Sue and Emily, who
e on duty that day. Emily had been working on Saturday and gave a
ourful account of the day's events. Things had started off slowly but had
ed up in the afternoon when they had several donations in and had had to
help moving things downstairs. Liz had always stressed the importance of
oing the shop floor clear and was glad to hear that they had taken this to
rt. They chatted over coffee and Liz heard the latest news of their friends
 families. It was part of her job to provide support to the volunteers, many
hom were widowed or divorced, and lived alone. They were on the whole a
rful lot and there were many laughs as well as some sad tales. Mrs
edith's daughter and son-in-law had brought in some of her things. They
 how much their mother had enjoyed her visits to the shop, and had wanted
things to be given to it.

k downstairs, Liz got on with her job. She looked around.
 last I'm winning,' she thought. She opened the next bag; the contents
ed familiar. Surely she had seen that jacket before, and that hat. Liz sighed
he remembered who had worn them, yes, Mrs Meredith. She continued
tying the bag; shoes, jumpers, skirts, all immaculate. Then she found the
ers, well worn. As she felt inside them she discover a little packet. Opening
 found a bundle of notes. She took them out and counted them. Five
dred pounds.
ow!' she thought. After labelling the packet and putting it in the safe she
d Emily to come downstairs.
 you recognise these?' she asked, pointing at the slippers.
s, they belonged to Mrs Meredith. She was wearing them the last time I saw

anks, Emily. Do you know where her daughter lives?'
ink she lives in Prescott Place. I'll find out for you.'
anks again, Emily. What do you know about the family?'

'Her daughter is called Amy. She's married, and has a son who is bright and very anxious to go on a school trip to France. They're hard up. Her husband kidney trouble, and often has to take time off work.

'Thanks Emily. I'll tell you later why I want to know.'

When she went to see Mrs Meredith's daughter, Liz took the slippers with h

'Do you recognise these?'

The woman caught her breath,

'Yes, they belonged to my mother.'

'May I come in?'

'Of course, please do.'

Over a cup of tea Liz told the whole story.

'I'll have to get you to sign for the money. Perhaps you could come back to t shop with me.'

Back in the shop, the story was told once again. Liz was glad that her detect work had paid off, and wondered if Mrs Meredith's grandson would go to France.

ichael Orton

chael was born in Hove, Sussex, just before World War II, and can just nember skies full of German planes. Michael, his mother, and their dog ved for the duration of the war to his grandparents home in Leicester. ucated at Hove College (a minor Public School) and Brighton Technical llege, Michael was accepted for a scientific apprentice scheme with the mic Weapons Research Establishment (AWRE), Aldermaston. He trained a health physicist and continued his career with the Ministry of Defence, the ntral Electricity Generating Board, Nuclear Electric Plc, and British clear Fuels Ltd. In Wales, Michael was a member of Rhinog and South wdonia Search and Rescue Team for 21 years. He started dabbling in nputers in 1961, worked with the STRETCH Supercomputer at AWRE, has l internet access since 1988, and is a member of the Softwear Development up of IT Wales His studies have also included Public Relations. Michael l his wife Shirley, both of whom are Ambulance First Responders in rlech, have four children, eight grandchildren and a great-grandson.

17
One Woman's Wars

he Jewish Holy Day of Yom Kippur in October 1973 started as any other day for Rivkah, a twenty-year-old Jewish housewife and David, her sband.

avid hadn't gone to the Kol Nidre service the previous evening, and they e not planning to go to any of the services on the day. They were not fasting l they lay in bed listening to Voice of America and the BBC Overseas Service, he normal Israeli programmes were not broadcasting during the holiday.

ey lived in a block of flats in the middle of Hazor, built on the lical site set in hilly country in north Galilee. Their flat looked out over a are dominated by a Soviet T-34 tank that sat in the middle of a flowerbed, ced there as a memorial to those who gave their lives defending the town ing the War of Independence in 1948.

vid was a Major in an armoured brigade, and, when not on active duty with Israeli Defence Forces (IDF), was a science teacher at a school in nearby ed.

fed had become well known to Christians, as 'A City on the hill that could be hid', from the Sermon on the Mount. His parents had helped to defend ed when, in 1947, Fourteen thousand Arabs attacked it. The Arab mander had promised to make the area Jew-Free by Passover that year, and they were fighting for their survival. Then a miracle had happened. Less than two thousand people, some elderly and some really only children, togeth with six hundred Israeli Palmach troops, had defeated and thrown the Arabs from the town.

When he grew up, David fought in the Six-Day War, his tank had been one o the first to fight its way onto the Golan plateau.

Rivkah had done her initial training in the Army Military Intelligence Corps and, though married, had stayed on and sought further promotion, hoping th this would lead to further support for sponsored University Education. She ha specialised in secure radio communications and had recently been promoted Junior Intelligence Officer. When not involved with the IDF, Rivkah worked i a local branch of a large Israeli Bank.

Early in the afternoon their lives were shattered when sirens started to soun They tuned the transistor radio to Kol Israel and found that it was already broadcasting in spite of the High Holiday. To their horror they heard that Isra was being attacked by both Syria and Egypt, and the attack had started at around 14.00hrs, less than half an hour before. David phoned his base camp, near the main road from Tiberius to Kyriat Shemona, and got all the details.

Looking very serious, he put down the phone and turned to Rivkah.

'The Army Northern Command HQ says that massive Syrian and Egyptian forces have attacked in the north and south. Again we are to fight for our live. Rivkah, why did it have to happen to us now? I love you so much.'

Soon Phantoms and Skyhawks roared overhead on their way to the Golan battleground.

Rivkah grabbed her uniform, her UZI and her rucksack. She stuffed four spa 30-round clips into the side pockets of her combat trousers. David had taken his M-16 carbine from the wardrobe, and fixed two duplex magazines to the butt with thick rubber rings.

David drove them both to the large military base on the road from Hazor to Tiberius. When they arrived, there were soldiers everywhere; lorries, tanks, APCs were all being prepared for action. A long line of military vehicles, including modified dune buggies with TOW anti-tank missiles, had already started to leave for the battlefield in a straggling convoy. Ambulances were rushing from the battlefront to the nearest hospitals.

David met up with some of his colleagues, and they raced off to Golan in someone's car.

Rivkah was only able to get in a quick 'Shalom. Keep safe darling', as he dro off.

She just stood there, in a state of shock, for several minutes. After a little wh the sirens sounded again, and this brought her back to reality. All around div for cover, but the aircraft roaring overhead were Israeli, returning from the battlefield to rearm.

She reported to the main office, which was in chaos. Soon she and two othe girls, who were also in Intelligence, were seconded by a General and told to t

orry loaded with radio gear to the Arik Bridge on the Jordan river, just above
e point where it joins the Sea of Galilee. The general wanted to set up his
ward command post there. The bridge was a narrow iron girder affair, but it
s strong enough to take a tank. However tanks were not something that the
neral had in any quantity. He only had two and they were old Shermans, still
ed with the 75mm gun, and useless against the Russian supplied tanks that
vkah knew they would have to face. With only a few cars and two buses, he
s only able to find two hundred men to take to the bridge.

ust over the bridge the General set up his HQ, using the Radio lorry, with
vkah in charge as Intelligence Officer, as there was nobody more senior or
h the right training or experience there at that time.

ne General was determined to hold the bridge at all costs, as this was the last
ensive line before the enemy were in the heartland of Galilee, and there the
ks would be attacking civilians. The death toll was bound to be high. There
re growing signs of panic amongst the IDF top brass. It had already been
ggested that anti-tank weapons be issued to the civilian population in Galilee,
l that Tiberius, Hazor and Safed be evacuated.

t the same problem presented itself as in the war of Independence. Where
s it safe to evacuate to? All Israelis were in the front line, and there was no
e haven to evacuate them to, even if there were time and transport.
mehow, the Syrians had to be stopped at the Jordan River. The messages
t were coming in were very confusing, with Syrian Tanks and APCs being
orted everywhere.

on four busloads of soldiers from different units had arrived, some in part
form only, with sneakers, T-shirts and even Beach Shorts, and, by way of
trast, Yom Kippur best suits and prayer shawls. The General decided to
d them out to see what they could find, and after they had driven about
ee miles in a mixture of military and civilian vehicles, they reported contact
h the enemy.

the same time Rivkah received a message that elements of an elite IDF
gade were being attacked from the rear. She took the initiative and
tacted both units, and after exchanging radio messages, the two groups
ped firing at each other.

th groups then decided to withdraw, without consulting the General, and
n he had to stand on the Bridge and stop them, and order them forward
in. 'Kadee-mah,' (forward), he kept on saying; and for the next day he stood
re personally directing the troops into battle as they arrived, not bothering
rmuch as to which units they belonged. His initiative was to save Israel's
thern front.

ne situation during the night was even more confused as the Syrians
tinued to move forward. The airforce had virtually been withdrawn from the
t, as it was taking very heavy, unsustainable losses from Surface-to-Air
siles, which were proving impossible to jam. One senior officer reported

that he had bumped into an advancing column of Syrian tanks, and had only just managed to escape, and this was only because he spoke Arabic so well tha he had been able to convince them that he was Iraqi! At Nafeq, a large tank park in the centre of the Golan, the Syrians came in on one side as the Israeli soldiers arrived in buses and cars on the other side, and there was hand-to-hand fighting. The situation was dramatically changed when the commander a lone Israeli Centurion tank saw what was happening, and joined at the rear the attacking tanks, shooting at close range right into the magazines of the Syrian weapons. Out of an attacking force of about two dozen tanks, this lone Centurion accounted for over a dozen.

Soon after dawn on the second day, Rivkah got a nasty shock; thirty to forty tanks appeared on the skyline behind the bridge. They were clearly Syrian T-62's. They opened fire, but before they could get the range they were attacked by IDF Skyhawks and Phantoms, and without infantry, anti-aircraft, or missi support, the crews jumped out and ran, leaving the thirty-five tanks, some wi their engines still running. Soon, the General had these tanks dug in as fixed anti-tank guns to protect the bridge.

An hour later, shells suddenly began to arrive in the area, and the Israeli personnel dived into ditches and trenches. They didn't know it, but a Syrian Ranger unit, with a forward Artillery Control Officer, had infiltrated into the hills overlooking the Israeli troops, during the night. Rivkah felt fairly safe; there was an IDF Major behind her and the two girls and two other soldiers i her trench. Then the enemy changed to airburst shells and one exploded righ above them.

The Major behind her was killed, the side of his head torn off by the shrapne and Rivkah was hit by two fragments. She was lying on her left side, with her hands over her ears, when one piece hit her right thigh, gouging out a ragged lump of flesh. The other hit her right upper arm and then tore into her right breast, striking her ribs, breaking three, and sending bone fragments into her chest cavity. She felt a violent blow to her chest; then incredible pain, followe by difficulty in breathing. She was covered in blood from her own wounds an from the blood that had spurted from the fatal head wounds to the Major.

Using a radio the General called for Medics. Before they arrived, a third yea medical student was able to put an improvised chest drain valve in Rivkah using a tube from a water bottle and a bayonet, to try to drain the blood and that was causing her lungs to collapse. She was very fortunate, that before hi medical studies, he had been a US Army Combat Medic.

Counter battery fire soon silenced the Syrian guns, and a helicopter arrived Rivkah was fitted with a proper Heimlich chest drain valve, and could breath properly again. She was now being given oxygen, which helped. However because of Rivkah's respiratory problems they were unable to give her morp She was flown by helicopter to the nearest surgical unit and intubated; that the last thing she could remember. After emergency surgery, Rivkah was tak by ambulance, together with three seriously wounded male soldiers, to th mbam Hospital in Haifa, not far from the Railway and Bus Stations towards ifa Port. There she underwent further surgery, and when she had recovered m the anaesthetic, she was told that she would need extensive plastic surgery her leg, arm, and chest, but that the end result was expected to be isfactory. She would end up with a silicone implant to replace the damaged sue that the doctors had had to remove from her right breast.

s Rivkah lay in her bed in the Ramban Hospital, she wondered if her sband was alive. All that was known was that Israeli casualties had been very h. Because of the confusion at the battlefront, nobody really had any firm vs. Staff had told Rivkah that the Syrians had been held at a great cost in n, planes, and tanks, and that it was rumoured that General Moshe Dayan l activated Israel's secret nuclear force, to prevent it from being over-run by enemies. PM Golda Meir had been on TV and Radio, promising that the ple of Israel would fight and live. It also soon became clear that the Arab diers were not as committed as their leaders to the destruction of the Jewish te. As soon as the battle turned in Israel's favour, they began to run. Their ders were far from the battlefront, hiding in shelters.

n the hospital ward it was now common knowledge that America was ifting munitions and aircraft from Europe and direct from America. Then e the shock news that US President Richard Nixon had declared a state of FCOM-2, one state of alert short of war, when he had been informed, ngly as it later transpired, that the Russians were sending forces to the area. they all gathered around the radio, Rivkah's greatest worry was that the ation would get so bad that Israel would be forced to use its nuclear pons to survive. She was afraid that this might be the start of WW-3, with death of tens of millions. It became very clear to Rivkah that Military lligence had made a major mistake in not warning of this massive attack on el by forces that had more tanks than NATO and more soldiers that the l population of Israel. Rivkah took it personally. She was an Officer in Army lligence, and it was they, and also Israel's Foreign Intelligence Service, ssad, that had missed the signs. By their errors, the lives of five million Jews been put at risk. Perhaps, she thought, Israel's unacknowledged nuclear ke force might, after all have to be used to save them all.

was to be over a week later when she finally heard that David had survived. was in a hospital in Safed, after suffering burns when his tank was hit in a ce battle with Iraqi tanks on the Golan Heights. His tanks, she heard, had n involved on one of the largest tank battles since World War Two, and their ory ensured that not only had the Golan front held, but they had been able rive the Syrian tanks back towards Damascus. On the Golan, they had royed more Syrian tanks than the UK owned.

a result of her many stays in hospital undergoing further plastic surgery, ah lost much of her characteristic bright sparkle, and, after the war, her riage to David didn't go well.

To help with her post-traumatic stress, and at the army's expense, Rivkah enrolled in an IT Security course. This seemed to help her initially but, after many setbacks and reconciliations, David and Rivkah finally separated.

Rivkah eventually left her beloved Israel and came to England, to distant family members in Manchester. The Manchester Branch of her Bank wanted staff with her IT skills, and the pay was very good. In Manchester, Rivkah worked in her spare time doing Public Relations work for Israel. She went on many training courses with her bank and became expert in IT security and the prevention of banking fraud. The rapid growth of IT systems and credit card use had changed Banking. It was her skills that were needed to try to reduce high-tech crime, which was becoming unmanageable. It was at a meeting in Manchester that she had met up with Mickey, an ex-Aldermaston scientist with very radical ideas on the use of nuclear weapons. He was to have a lasting effect on her life.

At last it seemed that Rivkah had found her niche in life. For almost two decades she lived, and worked in her well-paid job, in Manchester. She had many acquaintances but few close friends, except Mickey, who was happily married with children. This life seemed as if it could go on forever, but in September 2001, Al-Qaida attacked America with hijacked aircraft, killing thousand people.

Now America was even more involved in the war of Islamic Terrorists against the West, 'The War on Terror.' Al-Qaida had done something that Rivkah never thought possible. It had got the USA fighting in the Israeli trenches against Islamic Terrorism. The horrible events of 9/11 also changed her life for good. Israel was yet again in danger, and needed her skills back home.

In late 2002, she left the Bank, and England, to return to Israel to work in Israeli Government Service. This led to another life changing event; in 2005 married a senior Government Official whose wife had died from cancer two years earlier. Rivkah was now a stepmother to two children, and settled down to her ready-made life, both as Government Employee and stepmother.

Rivkah wondered if her two step-children would have to fight in future war or would the badly kept 'secret' of Israel's nuclear capacity bring relative peace to the troubled Middle East? Perhaps not peace, but perhaps 'Jihad tomorrow never Jihad today,' might be the best that she could hope for.

She did keep in contact with old friends in the UK, especially Mickey, the ex-AWE Aldermaston physicist, who had been an expert on the use of nuclear weapons and their effects. Rivkah often e-mailed him when she wanted information on the effects of WMDs. He believed that peace would come to the area when the Arabs came to recognise that there was a terrible price to pay a Jew-Free 'Palestine;' an Arab-free radioactive desert! She sometimes shuddered to think of his views on the use of such weapons.

As the new century entered the middle of its first decade, Rivkah became increasingly involved with the Iranian threat to the very survival of Israel from Ahmadinejad's suspected covert nuclear weapons programme. Rivkah had s ny satellite pictures of the underground facilities at Natanz, the Isfahn anium Conversion plant, and the Parchin test facility and research labs. She d attended many meetings on the threat and had even been part of an Israeli egation, which, in August 2006, had held meetings with British Intelligence, London, on the Iranian Question. She also had attended meetings with US elligence officials. But all those meetings with the USA and the UK had ieved nothing, only vague Security Council Resolutions that had little effect. e Iranian Threat had changed all their lives at work. There was a deadly eat to Israel's very existence from Ahmadinejad, Iran's new leader.

s she looked out of her office window, she could see the beautiful hills and untains of Judea and Samaria and the new tower blocks that had recently n built in the suburbs of Tel Aviv. Tel Aviv was a thriving City in a thriving intry; a secret nuclear super-power that she had helped to survive, in the st troubled part of the world. A world of 5 million Jews in a hostile sea of 175 lion Arabs and Persians, who made no secret of their desire to throw them into the sea. She hoped and prayed that the future would bring them peace ast, rather than the alternative of a multi-million-death nuclear war.

nd she had changed too. She and her new ready-made family were now ular members of the local Synagogue. They now kept Kosher and all the y Days. At last she felt herself a part of Eretz Israel, the State of Israel, that had fought so hard to defend.

18
Luther the Dachshund

L*uther, the standard dachshund, is a short-legged, elongated sausage-dog of the hound family.*

The breed's name is German and literally means 'badger dog,'

Looking at Luther, asleep on silk cushions, with his little legs up the air, you wouldn't associate him with a hunting dog.

However, the standard size was developed to scent, chase and flush badgers and other burrow-dwelling animals, while the miniature version was to hunt rabbits.

Dachshunds come in three sizes. A full-grown standard dachshund averages 16 to 28 lbs, while the miniature variety typically weighs less than 11 lbs. The Kaninchen weighs 7-9 lbs. I have never seen a Kaninchen myself. The three sizes all look the same, apart from the size!

Luther is a five year old black and tan, curly haired standard. he weighs about 25 lbs.

'A dachshund is a half-dog high and a dog-and-a-half long,' which is their m claim to fame, although many poems and songs refer to them as 'two dogs long.'

Dachshunds have a wide range of colours. Black, Gold, and various mixture are common. Light-coloured dachshunds usually sport green or blue eyes rather than brown. They can also have eyes of two different colours; in rare cases, such as the double-dappled coloration dachshunds can have a blue an brown eye.

Luther has brown eyes.

Dachshunds come in three coat varieties. The most common is the smooth coated dog. This looks like a miniature Doberman-Pincher. The next mos recognised is the long coat –

Like Luther, who looks like a spaniel whose mother took thalidomide.

The wire-haired dachshund is least common; I have seen them and no recognised the breed.

Dachshunds are playful, fun dogs, known for their propensity to chase sma animals, birds and tennis balls, with great determination and ferocity. Man dachshunds are strong-headed or stubborn, making them a challenge to trai

Luther can be a right little bugger!
He can fold up his legs and refuse to budge. Grabbing his harne is then a useful way to grab hold of him!

achshunds have been known to have a liking for digging holes in the garden.
ough their legs are very short, they are very powerful. Dachshunds have a
ticularly loud bark, making them good watchdogs.
uther doesn't often bark, but when he does he sounds very
gressive.

ather is very laid back, and is the canine version of the typical
unge lizard.

achshunds have traditionally been considered a symbol of Germany, despite
ir pan-European heritage. Political cartoonists commonly used the image of
dachshund to ridicule Germany. The stigma of the association was revived
lesser extent during World War Two, though it was comparatively short-
d. German Field Marshal Rommel was known for keeping dachshunds.
toons depicting Hitler as a dachshund, with raised arm, exist. Perhaps not
unny as Basil Fawlty though! The official mascot for the 1972 Summer
mpics, hosted by Germany, was a dachshund with the name Waldi.

e flap-down ears and famous curved tail of the dachshund have deliberately
n bred into the dog. In the case of the ears, this is so that grass seeds, dirt
other matter do not enter into the ear canal. The curved tail is dual-
posed: so that the dog can be seen more easily in long grass and, in the case
urrowing dachshunds, to help haul the dog out if it becomes stuck in a
row.

ey adapt their skills to forage for food in the modern house and can open
rs with their front paws. A standard one can easily reach a door handle
n standing on its back legs.
ather is very partial to margarine, and he will jump onto the
ing table to grab a tub of it. He thinks that all tins contain dog
d, and will lick and drool over any tins in the car from the
kly trip to Lidl or Tesco.
ther loves 'walkies in car,' and will rush to the front door as
n as my wife, Shirley, collects the shopping bags.

ther seems to be playful, but his favourite game is to lie on his
k with his paws in the air.
s is a reflection of their original purpose though. Having been bred at one
t as Wild Boar hounds, the dogs have a tendency to roll on their backs. This
behaviour' has rather warlike origins. The dog would be sent into the
rgrowth to flush out the boar. The boar would, upon seeing the smaller
al, give chase. The dog would lead the boar towards the huntsman,
reupon it would throw itself upon its back. The boar would then pass over

the dog, who would then attempt to attack the throat or the genitalia of the passing boar; wounding the boar sufficiently for the huntsmen to kill their pr

For his size, Luther has a large mouth and very large teeth.

Luther was brought up in Southampton, but his first owner died and we took him over when he was five years old.
Surprisingly, when he first encountered badger tracks in North Wales, where he now lives, he got excited and followed them.

Luther can run fast for his size, but he runs in a funny sort of w it's really a series of jumps, with his tail held up like a flagpole. F tail reminds me of films of Al-Qaida warriors on horseback carrying their flags in Afghan terror training camps. Actually hi running is rather more like a horse than a dog.

For a dog of his size Luther has very thick bones. his spine feel like that of an adult human, and his leg bones seem the same thickness as a welsh sheep dog.

Even young children can recognise Luther as 'the sausage dog.'

Luther is really a big dog in a small package.

Sadly, just a few days before we had finished compiling thi anthology, Luther had a stroke and died. Even though most of only knew Luther through the amusing stories of his escapade told to us by Michael Orton, we all feel as if we have lost a frier

19
The Elderberry Tree.

uring the war my mother and I left Sussex and went to Wigston, just
outside Leicester, to stay with my Grandparents. I left the house late
mer 1939 with my mother and Pluto, the labrador. Two nights before, we
ked north and saw flames on the horizon as London was bombed.

xt door lived some German Jewish Refugees. They had a small baby. The
after the bombing they packed up, left the house, and went north. They had
e with nothing, and I remember that my mother had to lend them a drawer
ut their baby in.

y mother packed a suitcase and took Pluto and myself to Wivelsfield Railway
ion. There were no buses or taxis so we all had to walk. I could only carry
toys in a shopping bag. Because of bomb damage, we were stopped at
tersea and we had to go by bus to St Pancras Station. We saw smoke and a
e bomb crater when we arrived at the Station.

e arrived in Leicester in the dark and at Grandma's, unexpected.

e stayed there all through most of the war, except for short stays in
ykinler when my father was stationed at the nearby Hollywood barracks,
later in Cleethorpes.

e late summer, probably in 1940, Grandma took me on a walk across the
ls not far from her house. We were to pick blackberries, but at that time
e were few; most had been picked, and anyway the season was coming to an
. But grandma found an Elderberry tree, full of hanging bunches of ripe
ies. She picked enough to fill her bag, which was of crocheted white string
a green lining. She made an Elderberry tart, and it was very nice. For the
few days she went back to the tree and repeated the harvesting. For the
three or four years she did the same when the summer came to an end.

May 8th 1945 we left Leicester and travelled by train to London. My father
managed to arrange a short leave to come with us. The streets were full of
le Celebrating VE-Day. It took us most of the day to cross London to
oria Station and get a train to Burgess Hill Station, and then go by taxi to
old home. We had my pet Dutch rabbit, James Whiskers, with us. When we
ack to the Sussex home it was very late.

ring the war it had been unoccupied, apart from a week or so in the
mer when we had come down to look after it. Pluto had died of old age
ng the war; he was about twelve when he died. Now my only pet was James
skers.

weeds were much higher than I was, and the shrubbery was just a jungle.
electricity had been disconnected and we only had a gas ring. Fortunately
ad an old brass duplex oil lamp. This was our only form of lighting, apart

from candles. Perhaps that is why I started collecting oil lamps in the 1970s a now have a collection of over forty.

There was nothing to eat in the garden, but along the back fence were three very large elderberry trees, in flower. Two were very close together, and years later I built a tree-house in them. They were next to a large laburnham tree.

In early June my mother cleared a small piece of garden and planted some outdoor tomato plants. Later we had plums from the Victoria plum tree and some himalayan blackberries, and later still huge numbers of elderberries from the three large trees at the back of the garden. At about this time my father w demobbed.

Years later, in the late 60s, I came to Harlech and found elderberry trees ne the house that I had bought. They were growing in a wet patch in the wood behind my house.

I then started to make elderberry wine. At first it was in 1 gallon demijohns. Now I have my own trees, over a dozen of them, some almost twenty feet tall now make five gallons of elderflower wine and another five gallons of elderberry wine. I managed to obtain several plastic five-gallon containers which are just ideal for that purpose.

At present, I am totally self-sufficient for elderflowers, but because of the b from the woods behind my house, I have to collect elderberries from variou other places.

Anglesey is rich in elderberry trees, so I always arrange to visit my daughte early September, equipped with a plentiful supply of plastic bags.

Each year my own trees grow bigger and produce more fruit. I hope eventu to be self–sufficient in both elderflowers and elderberries. And I keep experimenting with ways to deter the birds from picking MY elderberries.

Elderberry is my favourite red wine. Perhaps it is due to Grandma's elderbe tarts all those years ago

ary Howell

*ry tells us she was born with many advantages, most of which she turned
back on. Educated to be a lady at a private convent, she excelled at
ancy and achieved fifty-two A star A levels. Her university career, and her
rsing career, both ended abruptly with spells in prison. Both times she was
ased without stain. She has lived all over the world, with as many aliases
overs. Among those lovers she numbers the Aga Khan and the Acond of
at. She has been, an orthodontist's assistant, a serial absconder, sawn in
f by a magician and a happily married mother of three. Very occasionally,
ry is known to tell fibs. Mary has also been published in 'the Guardian'
spaper*

20
Germaine Greer Ruined My Life

am proud of my independence, personal preference though, my sister's been
married for years. She's got four children, five if you count her husband. I
w it's an old joke, but it's true. He's more trouble that the kids, and not even
eful. Just expects his socks washed, his dinner ready, and free sex. My sister
s telling me I don't know what I'm missing.

ck tock, tick tock,' she says when I go too far.

s to remind me of my biological clock winding down fast as I hurtle towards
ty. Her kids *are* lovely, but I have a life mapped out; a career and a
tgage to think about and I don't want to be a kept woman.

e *Female Eunuch* was book of the week recently on *Radio Four*. GG was
g interviewed about it. She didn't sound nearly as radical as her reputation.
s intrigued, and thought it high time that I read the book, to see what has
ged for the MIW (Modern Independent Woman).

ent to the local library. I didn't think the book would still be on the shelves
asked the librarian. I always go straight to the desk and ask them to look; it
s time. To be precise, it saves me time. Or at least it usually does.

librarian studied the screen for a moment.

ere's nothing listed.'

just the author's name.' I switched to helpful mode.

w do you spell it?'

ll, I ask you!)

R E E R.'

, I'm still not getting anything on the screen.'

s I found hard to believe.

at's the book called again?'

I repeated it, thinking little light bulbs might start switching on in the librarian's head.

(Oh, that Germaine GREER, why didn't you say so?)

'How are you spelling eunuch? Is it N U N I K?'

(Oh my god, how can anyone get 'nunik' from eunuch?)

'It definitely starts with EUN then?'

I'm not certain whether it's an O, or is that Enoch? It can't be an A surely?

I hesitated.

By this time, quite a queue was forming. I glanced in their direction. I am always utterly delighted if I am the cause of a bottleneck. I love to think of the all toe-tapping, mentally listing things they would rather be doing, and directing evil looks at me.

I smiled. Not the smug smile I was feeling, but my brilliant smile. There was disconcertingly good-looking man standing next to me.

The suavest of voices oozed from the Alpha Male and he looked straight into my eyes.

'It's U.'

'Me?'

My knees weakened.

'I've got it now,' the librarian broke the spell, 'I can have it here within a wee It will cost you fifty pence, though.'

'That will be fine.'

'Your name please?'

I spelled it immediately, switching to super helpful mode. Even I was beginning to feel that I might be trying the queue's patience.

'Address?'

I never like saying the name of my house aloud. It's embarrassingly awful. It came with the house and I haven't changed it. I would like to, but I'm rather superstitious and feel that it would be bad luck, like it's bad luck to change the name of a boat. It's my first house, my biggest step on the road to independence, and I have only lived there a few months. Besides, there must some reason for the name. Someone must have gone to a deal of trouble to think of it.

'I'll spell it,' I said, leaning in closer to the librarian.

I hissed each letter in a stage whisper, suspecting she would make a travesty it if left to her own devices.

'Raindrops on Roses?' said in a mixture of disbelief, scorn and her loudest voice.

'I know that house.'

The voice, and two lovely, blue eyes quite took my breath away.

I had never managed to picture honey dripping from the lips 'til this moment 'Oh?'

'I was born there.'

h?'

ave you lived there long?'

o.'

he house has a remarkable history. I could tell you about it over some coffee,
ou like.'

f all the moments to be lost for words it had to be that one.)

must have raised my eyebrows. He was quite defensive, and I could have
orn he was blushing.

's such a coincidence, that's all, to bump into the owner of my old home. I
here on holiday for the first time in years. Come back to show the children
ir roots.'

h.' I tried not to make it sound too flat.

e queue, now five deep, all leaned forward obligingly, like the Von Trapp
ily about to sing, and I noticed a remarkable similarity in their smiling
·s.

vould be delighted to have coffee with you, and it would be my pleasure if
came to the house.'

t one Alpha Male, but six. Come to think of it, Alpha One, apart from being
·ried already, was a little old for me, but Two, Three, Four, Five and Six…

independent existence ceased from that day, and it's all GG's fault.

21
White birds

He watched, captivated, as the white bird stretched her wings. Was she resting? Was she *en route* to far flung places? He was sure the bird was female; graceful and provocative, she waited near the pond in his garden. After the third day he began to think her display was for him, for his eyes only, so daintily did she stretch her neck to peck crumbs, or crane it to look over her sleek back, straight at him.

He was mesmerised.

The bird had deliberately chosen his garden; she was offering herself to him: he did not trap her she would fly away and he would lose her. He must at least try.

As he moved silently towards the bird with his blanket ready to throw over her, his breath was short, and he felt his heart would burst in his chest so great was his excitement. Just as he was close enough, the bird looked up in alarm. He saw panic in her eyes, then a darkening akin to loathing, as the bird realised her fate. He threw the blanket, covering her, as much to shut out the look as catch her. He was disappointed, angry even, that the bird had not resisted, that there had been no chase. She lay limply under his arm and he was tempted to wring her neck, but the thought of her beauty stayed his hand and he decided keep her, now that he had her.

He stuffed the warm mass of feathers into the wooden box he had handy, not stopping to look at her, concentrating on sealing her in. He noticed that she shrank away from him and, as he hammered the nails, he began to resent her. By the last nail the resentment had grown to hate. These were not the feelings he wanted, and he blamed the bird for them.

Not knowing what to do with the box, he left it there in the middle of the stone flagged kitchen. The back door was ajar, a shaft of sunlight slanting in, but the bird could not feel its warmth, only a wind blowing its scents and mysteries her: salt air (of course the house stood isolated near the sea), fishy and indeterminate foreign smells from Africa across Spain then France, redolent sultry, sensuous Saharan heat.

But the wind that should have gladdened the bird's heart; the wind that should take her wherever it was going, served only to awaken her desire for escape.

She could not open her wings in the box and the man did not heed her piteous cries. Sometimes he kicked the box to make the bird be quiet, so she took to closing her eyes, sleeping on her feet, only her mind soaring with dreams and memories.

Who could say what made the bird frantic for escape on that particular day? Perhaps the wind changed direction; perhaps the long 'V' of birds flying under the sun was calling her. From dawn she beat her wings against the sturdy box

re was barely room to unfurl but still she tried again and again, her beak
wing at the lid to widen the gap. White feathers streaked with blood fell
ugh the slats of the box and lay scattered on the cold, grey stone, the
ller ones travelling across the floor, taken by the wind, leaving red streaks.
bird's heart beat wildly. The exquisite pain, as her wings bloodied and
ke, if anything made her more frantic.

hen the man finally returned, or came down – it matters little whether he
been asleep or out fishing - the bloody feathers were a mess on his cold,
e floor. He thought a fox must have attacked his beautiful bird and he
ned to the box, but the lid was firmly in place. He prised it open. The bird,
naged and panting, now lay still in the bottom. He looked at her. Should he
g her neck and pluck the plump breast for a meal?
put his hand on her and the bird, too exhausted to flinch, was warm. The
d smelled metallic but did not disgust him; neither did the sight of the
ngled mess of the bird's wings. Tenderness welled within him. Grateful now
she would let him touch her, he did not feel in awe of her beauty as he had
e. He stroked her breast with his clumsy fingers; it was infinitely soft.
lecided he would care for her. He would make a leather collar with a long
chain for her slender neck. He could pull the chain whenever he wanted
May be she would lay eggs.

vas not long afterwards that a second bird appeared in his garden. This time
e was no sense of awe at the bird's beauty, no desire for possession,
ugh, after quite some time of watching, he felt sure this bird was waiting
im by the pond, where the wicket fence met the sand of the beach. He
ed out in his shirtsleeves and his gumboots, the sun catching on the
les of his braces, to shoo the bird away.
e man hesitated when the bird flew towards him as if to greet him, but was
surprised. It was as if there was business to attend to, man to man. The
nse of white wings momentarily blocked all else from sight, as if a soft,
e cloud had descended, filling his senses with the rush of wind and wings
ose to him. The surprise came with the force of the first touch; a blow to his
k. He thought the bird might have misjudged his distance and he put his
on his face to feel the smart. It stung where his fingers touched.
essive blows were harder; he reeled but the pain ceased to register. The
e of the thudding wings on his skull was loud. He tried to open his eyes to
for an escape but the white was replaced by red and still he could not see.
ut his arms over his head to cradle it, afraid to touch the rawness and gore
ne knew were there. He felt sharp stabbing pains up his arms as the bird's
broke the flesh and then the bones. His arms were flung up and held away
him, as if he were no more than a plaything, a rag doll, then dashed
tedly against something hard and abrasive like a wall. As he began to lose
ciousness; he imagined himself lying beside his sullen pet, in the only
of sunlight she could reach at the end of her chain. He no longer felt the

attack, though he knew it was not yet all over.

When, some days later, the man's body was found, it was assumed, from the extent of the injuries and the number of white feathers, that the man had bee attacked by several birds. Since no one knew of any relatives, or of any friend he might have, the house was shut up. Some of the voyeurs took mementos small items that could be secretly taken, such as a long filigree chain with small, broken collar, or larger items carried away brazenly. There was no reason to waste anything. People talked about the incident for a while, then interest and completely forgot that there even was a house still there. None o them particularly liked that part of the beach.

There was a report that a young couple with a baby used it as a squat for while. So they said, but nobody knew very much about them either.

*

A slip of a girl, puffing breath to blow a straggling fringe out of her eyes, so can see the sea beyond the wicket fence, stands with her hands plunged i soapy water. All up her arms, ugly scars; livid criss-crosses as if some terribl accident has befallen her. Looking at her beautiful face it would be hard t imagine the wounds are self-inflicted, born of a desperate need. The pain, ea time she had wielded the knife, making her mind soar, taking her to heights happiness and freedom, until the blood, the anger and the dull pain of her li returned her to her self. She no longer thinks of them. Only sometimes does run her fingers over her arms, feeling the ridges and troughs, and remember

A baby cries and she turns from the sink to a man at the table, reading newspaper, his head is down; he is concentrating and has not heard the tin cry. It has not made his gut contract or his breasts tingle as if a hot iron wer pressing the inside, as milk is released, leaving two small, round, damp pate

She looks at the triangle of taught flesh, where the buttons of the check shi she ironed lovingly earlier that morning remain open.

'Pete.'

She calls him gently, her gut contracting, not with pain as before, but a stir desire for his gentle hands and his whispering voice, wanting him to look u she can see the handsome face break into the slow, spreading smile when sees her; so he would come and put his arms protectively round her in a wa comforting hug, and kiss her hair, her neck, anywhere she presented to him

The baby's cry is lustier and Pete reluctantly raises his eyes from the pape and laughs when he sees her looking at him.

'Has she been crying for a while?'

He goes to the baby in the next room and picks it up as tenderly as if it we his own. She sees him in the doorway, filling the frame, the baby cradled in arms, and smiles at the look on his face.

*

en Sandra and David drove from the city to spend a long weekend by the
buying a place of their own was the last thing on their mind, until they saw
abandoned cottage, silhouetted against the evening sky, just before turning
ar to make their way back to the hotel.

t's take a look,' Sandra had said and, to please her, David had agreed.
e house looked forlorn.

could be wonderful,' Sandra padded down the wooden path from the wicket
e.

e gate swung open, half off its hinges.

e rubbed sand and grime off the windows and tried to peer in through the
d hole she had made.

esn't look like there's been any one here for some time. It's almost empty.'
e tried the door and it opened. She looked round for David, expecting to see
lacid face ready to indulge her; not this time. Perhaps he had gone round
ack.

e pushed the door wide and, since she could see no-one, walked inside. It
surprisingly light; the only sunlight that entered fell in a shaft where the
opened. A sea breeze had picked up and seemed to blow straight in, filling
nostrils with mixed scents. She shivered and was about to call David to
e and look inside with her, when she thought she heard humming and
med he must have come in through another door. She walked quietly to the
room, the kitchen, where the humming was coming from.

he sink stood a girl, her profile towards Sandra, her hands, plunged into
y water, had bubbles up near the elbow where the girl had rolled her
es out of the way. The girl pushed a bit of stray hair out of her eyes with
ack of her hand, looking out of the window, then made a puffing sound
her lips and her fringe lifted and fell back down again.

aby cried and the girl turned her head, away from Sandra towards the
en table, where a young man, with a shock of dark curly hair, sat
entrating on a newspaper spread out on the table. The young man, no
than a boy, did not look up, carried on humming, and the girl did not say
hing.

hasn't heard the baby', Sandra thought.

e felt the devastating discomfort in her breasts as milk released. This
end, their first away since the baby had died and the first time she had not
ke crying, and now this; the pills she had been given at the hospital were
osed to have stopped this.

ere you are,' said David, coming to her where she stood by the sink and
ng his arms round her with a little squeeze.

starving, shall we go? We could eat in the hotel tonight. What do you
?'

blinked away her tears as he kissed the top of her head. He shifted his
t from one foot to the other so she swayed slightly and leant back into

him. He rested his chin on the top of her head and they both took in th
overgrown garden and the view beyond.

'I like this place.' She said. 'There's something about it.'

Over the meal, candles glowing, a soft murmur of other guests, the smell c
her perfume each time he breathed in, David's heart ached. Two glasses of r
wine, after a whole day in the sea air, and the turmoil of the last weeks had t
him. The hospital said that it happened sometimes that babies died. Th
inquest had revealed nothing and he did not like to think of the perfect littl
body slashed with surgeon's knives, though the image visited him most nigh

'Leave it a while; let things take their course and try again.'

The advice had filled him with quiet rage, at the time, and he had wanted t
shout at the obstetrician.

'That little house,' he said, laying his hand over Sandra's and gently strokir
'shall we see if it is for sale?'

The first smile and look of pleasure he had seen in weeks crossed her face.

'We could do it up. It would be a great hide away for weekends. It's not tha
from the city.'

The more he thought about it, the more he warmed to the idea.

Their enquiries were fruitless. The house belonged to no-one. The owner w
dead. The agents were vague or evasive. David and Sandra took to coming t
the village most weekends and gradually they did up the little house. Davi
mended the broken gate; they stripped floors, painted walls, collected
driftwood for fires. The project gave them a focus. Sandra lost her sad look a
began to regain her figure. David no longer thought nightly of the little gre
statue lying on a marble slab.

One evening, on the rag rug that Sandra had found in a junk shop, while th
light of the fire in the grate that David had cleaned spread warmly over the
bodies, they let things take their course. David smiled as he remembered th
consultant's words. Releasing grief, feeling joy, they conceived a girl.

The following morning, Sandra opened the door letting in a shaft of sunlig
breathed in the sweet smell of the sea, humming to herself. Outside two larg
white birds had stopped to drink water from the pond on their long flight sc
Sandra called softly to David to come and look, turning to him at the table f
the pleasure of seeing how his face would break into a smile as he looked up
her. He stood behind her, his arms surrounding her in a comforting hug.

'Aren't they beautiful?'

He kissed the top of her head, her soft neck, breathed in her perfume and c
not reply, wanting to stay like this forever.

ane Andrews

ne was born in Birmingham, and as one of six children enjoyed a very
py childhood. She attended Somerville and Marlborough (sadly not the
ord College, nor the Public School), but Somerville School, and
lborough Road School, in Small Heath. On leaving school Diane worked
telephonist with the G.P.O., whilst attending Kingsbury Road College
a week. She left the G.P.O. for adventure – in Guernsey! – as a waitress!
ved the island but hated the job; so, she returned home and worked for
ve years in telecommunications, for the Civil Aviation Authority at
ningham Airport – and loved every minute of it. She married Graham,
two special children John and Kate, moved to Barmouth in 1988, and
to Ynys in 1990. She has been working for Social Services for the last
teen years.

22
Age of Invisibility

atilda sat in the bus shelter, out of breath and furious. She was certain
that the driver had seen her hurrying for the bus, but he had pulled away
the kerb, seconds before she got there. *'When,'* she wondered, *'had she
lenly become invisible.'* She knew that if she had been young, pretty, and in
ni skirt, she would have been seated aboard the bus by now, - or was she
being cynical?

en she had first used her bus pass, the drivers would ask to see it, and look
iringly at how well she carried her years; but of late, they barely glanced as
climbed aboard, and never even looked at her bus pass. Even her children
ed her with indifference, and her opinions, when offered, were mostly
red, even though she knew she had probably lived a lot fuller and more
esting a life than they had, including driving ambulances during the war.
young never appreciate the older generation,' she thought, and gave a big

following day, she decided it was time for some action to be taken. From
ideboard drawer she removed a hatpin which had belonged to her mother,
out it in her coat pocket as she left the house. As she was waiting at the bus
with a group of boisterous youths behind her, the bus drew up, and the
ns jostled their way past. Matilda deftly jabbed the hat pin into the nearest
side; the backside's owner turned, shouting at his mate, and Matilda
ed aboard, the picture of innocence, and thought to herself, *'serve him
.'*

next two weeks were to give Matilda a new lease of life. She walked with a
ose, and a new spring in her step. The only problem was that she knew she

was enjoying it too much, and on the days she didn't use the hatpin, she felt quite disappointed.

Her family also noticed her assertive attitude when she turned down their last-minute baby-sitting requests, saying that she had already made other plans. In the past she had always put them first, and cancelled whatever she was planning to do; now they muttered to each other, 'What on earth's got into mom?'.

Arriving home, after a day's shopping, Matilda put the kettle on and made a cup of tea, before settling down with the *Evening Mail*. She turned to the second page where the headline caught her eye: **Phantom Bottom Piercer Strikes Again**. She read the article quickly. I said that the police were examining CCTV footage, and hoped they would soon be able to apprehend the culprit.

'Oh dear,' thought Matilda, as she retrieved the hatpin from her coat pocket and placed it back in the drawer, *'that's the end of that then - but then again perhaps not. But better give it a rest for a while.'*

23
Taken for a Ride

Martha had been putting the last of her shopping into the boot of the car when a tall dark woman approached her, like a long lost friend, enquiring [who] she was, and asking about the family. But for the life of her, Martha could [not] place the woman. 'I must be having one of my senior moments,' she [thought], as she racked her brains to identify the stranger.

[Ev]entually the woman asked if she was passing through Springfield, and if so [coul]d she cadge a lift, as she had missed the three-thirty train.

[Ma]rtha felt unable to refuse and, after stowing the woman's shopping trolley [in th]e boot, set off on their journey.

[As] she was driving along, Martha was finding out all sorts of things about her [new]ly found friend whose husband, she was informed, had left her for a [che]ckout girl at Tesco's, and whose sixteen year old daughter, Chantal was [preg]nant, and had moved in with the boyfriend; but the woman assured her [she], herself, was coping, with the aid of her new toy-boy partner, who was [te]n years younger than she was.

[Th]e conversation became more and more surreal as the journey progressed. [Mar]tha heaved a sigh of relief when, thankfully, they were coming into [Spri]ngfield. Her travelling companion asked her to turn left at the church, [stra]ight on, and then next left...

['An]d here we are,' she said, as they came to a halt outside a row of new [bun]galows.

[Ma]rtha could not contain herself any longer, and, as she opened the boot to get [the w]oman's shopping trolley out, she said,

['I'm] very sorry, but I can't remember your name.'

['It's] Sandra,' the stranger replied.

['I st]ill can't place you,' said Martha.

['Do] you know, I don't think I know you either,' said Sandra, 'I must have been [mist]aken. Anyway, thanks for the lift. 'Bye.'

[Fla]bbergasted, Martha watched Sandra's retreating back,

['Wh]at a bloody cheek.' She said out loud.

24
Alice

Alice sits at the window watching, waiting and wondering, who will turn
today. With any luck, it will be the small cheerful blonde. God forbid th
it's the thin faced, dark haired girl who has the look of someone permanentl
sucking on a lemon.

Funny how their names escape her, yet she can still touch her toes at the ag
ninety-four; and she can remember the past as if it were yesterday.

Most of her waking hours, lately, seem like living in a veil of mist; occasion
lifting, and then descending again.

Alice is back in 1922, it's her twelfth birthday, and she's running into th
kitchen of their small terraced cottage, from school. Her mother tells her t
wash her hands, and that a surprise awaits her in the front room.

The surprise turns out to be a mahogany upright piano, and she thinks tha
will burst with happiness.

A man comes from Barmouth once a week to give her piano lessons; but af
eight weeks he leaves, shaking his head, after telling her mother that Alice w
be teaching him next, and that she is wasting her money.

Fast forward, and it's now 1943. The piano lessons have stood Alice in goo
stead; she entertains at the local pubs and hotels, and at the dances in th
Memorial Hall for the servicemen, always a glass of shandy perched on th
piano.

1949, Jack, her husband, is an R.A.C. patrolman, but times are hard, and A
still contributes to the household with money earned from playing the pianc

Never blessed with children of her own, Alice gives piano lessons to loc
children and, although enjoying their company, often thinks,

'It's nice to see them come, but at least I can hand them back.'

The gate creaks, and Alice is back in the present; nothing wrong with h
hearing, thank goodness. Her face creases into a smile; it's the blonde girl.

Mair comes through into the sitting room,

'Hello Alice, how about playing me a tune, and I'll make a start on your tea

Alice is already seated at the piano. Closing her eyes she's back in the o
Memorial Hall, and she begins to play.

25
Mavis Makes Waves

avis sat at her desk, putting all her personal belongings from the drawer into her bag.

e office was deserted; it was a Bank Holiday week-end and the rest of the f had left early. Peter, the office manager, had asked if she would lock up. knew what he thought - good old Mavis, general dogsbody, nobody to rush e to, part of the furniture in fact, she won't mind at all. But the problem that she did mind, and increasingly of late - very much.

e had worked for Bryce & Sons, as the wages clerk and book-keeper, for nteen years, and apart from a morning off six months ago for her mother's ral, had never missed a day.

er turning off the lights, she locked the door for the last time, and walked town where she had managed to get the last appointment at the dressers. Later, with a completely new style and colour , she emerged ng like a new woman,

d looking like one.' the hairdresser had remarked.

ving made her way to the car park, she gazed with pride at the brand new per van, waiting, with all her belongings already packed neatly away inside. ce & Sons were in for a shock on Tuesday when she failed to show up, and ven bigger shock at the end of the month when the auditors were due in for nnual audit. She had been steadily siphoning off sums of money for the six months, and with the proceeds from the sale of her mother's house, she had quite a substantial amount in her account, in her new name of Hazel . Who would have thought identity theft was so easy. New name, new life, thought as she climbed into the cab, and set the Sat Nav for Dover. She d be in France tomorrow, and wherever else she decided to go after that, freedom.

26

The Dancing Policeman

It had all started with a small ad in the *Manchester Evening News* – 'Wanted: Mature Male with good Social Skills and Ability to Dance. Inclu lots of travel.' He had replied, mainly out of curiosity, and the sheer boredom his present life.

Now, George Dixon, ex-policeman (his name had been the source of much mirth over the years when he had still been in the force), was on the train do to Southampton to join the cruise ship *'Ariadne'*.

Arriving at Southampton he booked into a hotel for the night, and the following morning made his way down to the docks with trepidation, and hi boarding pass. Once there, he was told to report to Steve, the entertainment officer, in the Neptune Lounge where his duties would be explained.

The main part of his job was to keep the older matrons happy by inviting th to dance, and engaging in polite chit chat, but there was to be no over-familiarity. Also, a space of at least six inches was to be maintained between him, and the woman he was partnering, whilst they were dancing.

His fellow dancers were then introduced to him. Frank, a retired dairy farm from Somerset; Dai, a redundant steelworker from Port Talbot; and Sean, fr Ireland, who had a distinct air of mystery about him, and whose cabin he wo be sharing. They told him the job was a doddle, with wonderful food, and tha they were all veterans at cruising the Med. His predecessor Tim, had, apparently, danced off with a wealthy widow in Funchal, on the last cruise, a not been heard of since. On being shown his cabin, which was on F Deck in bowels of the ship, he felt rather disappointed, but was sure there would be of compensations.

After a wonderful lunch and a stroll on deck, he was given a grand tour of t ship to familiarise him with the layout. It was like a maze, and he was astonished at the size and opulence of the ship, and could imagine that it wa easy to get lost.

The following day the passengers came aboard, and George, with his fello dancers, went on deck to watch the brass band play the ship off from th quayside. 'This is the Life,' he thought.

The following afternoon he was initiated into his first tea dance in the mai ballroom. Approaching a sweet faced old dear, he was rebuffed with the rep that she would love to, but her legs were not quite up to it. On his third atte a buxom, jolly-hockey-sticks, matron rose to her feet, and they glided acros dance floor like two stately galleons 'as in the Joyce Grenfell song,' thoug George. Two hours later, and with great relief, the band finally packed up, a

rge and his fellow dancers retired to their cabins for an hour, to put their
up.

ve days elapsed; by this time George, with aching feet and a very queasy
nach after the Bay of Biscay crossing, was finding that the job was not all it
cracked up to be. Going ashore at the ports was the best part; it felt like
ig let out of a prison. No wonder most of the crew sucked peppermints; to
e the smell of the copious amounts of alcohol which they drank to numb the
edom, he supposed.

y the eighth day, the thought of one more rendition of Englebert
nperdink's, *Save the Last Waltz for Me,* made him want to throw himself
rboard, and the last port of call, Lanzarote, had been more like Lanzagrotty.
tering the ballroom that evening, he could scarcely believe his eyes; dancing
t closer than six inches, and in deep conversation with Sean, was, of all
ple, Celia French. It must have been nearly ten years since he had last seen
but she had hardly changed at all; still blonde and attractive, in a brassy,
ous way. During his career he had tried to nail her on several jewel
peries, but she had always managed to escape conviction, '*but not this time,*'
ight George.

erything slotted into place, the mysterious Stella Wise, who one of the
ards had told him about, who hadn't left her cabin since boarding at
thampton, was, of course, Celia. Then there were Sean's strange nocturnal
ts, and rumours of money and jewellery disappearing from cabins, during
ast few days.

made his way out of the ballroom to report his findings to the Captain.
rge obviously had not been employed just for his dancing skills. Then he
e his way back to the ballroom, hoping the next stop, Casablanca, would be
er – or else he might think seriously of jumping ship.

n well,' he sighed to himself, 'time for one more G&T, then back to the
-slow-quick-quick-slow.'

27
Why Me?

It was one of those scorching hot summer's days; the kind which we are occasionally lucky to get in July.

But unfortunately I was unable to enjoy it, seated, as I was, with twenty othe on orange plastic chairs, in a semi-circle, in a hall at the back of an old churc

I was attending a training course from work. Once upon a time the venues been nice hotels, with lunch laid on, but thanks to council cut-backs, we usu ended up in the church hall nowadays.

Even with all the windows open, the room was humid, oppressive and uncomfortable.

I was sandwiched between my two colleagues, Bethan and Anona. The latte kept crossing and uncrossing her legs; and, out of the corner of my eye, I cou see Bethan cleaning her watch with a safety pin. Looking around, I thought resembled a bunch of droopy wilting flowers, apart, that is, from Janet, th instructor, who looked as cool as a cucumber in her pale lemon frock. But ol her loud voice! It seemed exceptionally loud today, which was again unfortunate as I had a splitting headache.

My mind kept wandering, even though I was trying my utmost to concentra Then, suddenly, I heard my name being called from a distance. The next thin remember was being on the floor.

Bethan told me later that, on the whole, I had slipped quite gracefully off th chair, and although I had exposed a large amount of thigh, I hadn't quite revealed my knickers. This really was no comfort to me whatsoever.

Anyway, I digress, and back on the floor I could hear Janet telling everybod that I had only fainted, and to give me some air, and whilst I was down ther she might as well show them the recovery position. Oh, hadn't I explained? was attending a First Air Course. As she knelt down beside me I could smell perfume – *Poison* – mixed with perspiration. I opened one eye and saw that was alarmingly close.

'Please God,' I prayed, 'for goodness sake don't let her demonstrate the kiss life.'

28
Equilibrium

Whoever it was that said, visitors were like fish and went off after three days, certainly knew what they were talking about, Lydia thought.

...e was sat at the kitchen table, nursing a cup of tea which was now stone ...l. Her older sister, Jane, had taken up residence in the spare bedroom ...rly three weeks ago, and there were no signs of her leaving.

...e had arrived on the doorstep after a huge row with Sam, her husband, ...ng if she could stay for a couple of days.

...ice her arrival, a cloud seemed to have descended over the house. Tom, her ...band, when not at work, was spending most of his time in the greenhouse or ...pub, and the children, either in their bedrooms or out with their friends.

...e children called her, Jane the Pain, and Tom said Sam deserved a medal ...putting up with her all these years, as she was enough to make an angel ...n heaven swear - while using a few expletives of his own.

...eanwhile, Lydia had to listen to a diatribe of self pity, of all Sam's faults, and ...ow he had told Jane that she was a selfish, self-centred, drama queen, who ...y thought of one person, which, of course, was herself. Unfortunately, all of ...as true, and Lydia's patience was now wearing very thin.

...ell, something had got to be done, so having made a fresh cup of tea, she ...bed the stairs to confront Jane about how long she intended staying.

...e knocked the bedroom door, and walked in to find Jane putting the ...hed touches to her make-up.

...! I wondered where you had got to with my tea. You're late this morning.'

...lia resisted the temptation to pour the tea over her head, and replied, ...u're up early.'

...m rang me on my mobile, grovelling with his apologies, full of remorse, and ...ging me to go back. So I wondered if you could be a sweetie and possible ...o me back after breakfast.'

...course,' said Lydia through gritted teeth, 'it's only a fifty mile round trip.'

...'s remorse evidently didn't stretch to putting himself out to come and fetch

...ly good, I told Sam you wouldn't mind.'

...Lydia turned to go downstairs and give Tom the good news, Jane called

...the way, I hope you don't mind me saying, but Tom doesn't seem to spend ...h time at home, and don't you think it's rather unhealthy the way the ...ren spend all their free time in their bedrooms? I think it would be just as ...to keep a closer eye on them if I were you.'

...h that, Lydia finally lost her temper,

'Jane you are a rude, self-important and thoroughly nasty person; you have always been an awful elder sister; you are mean, and spiteful, and quite the worst person I have ever known; like everyone else, I can't think how Sam put up with you, and the only reason Tom escapes to the greenhouse, and the kids seek refuge in their bedrooms, is because you are such an abominable person be anywhere near; it will be a great relief to us all to see the back of you, and shall take you home with greatest of pleasure.'

Suffice to say, I think it will be quite a while before Jane visits again.

More importantly, Tom has ceased spending all his free time in the pub, and the children have emerged from their bedrooms - and peace reigns once more

Well, for the time being anyway.

rma Stockford

rma has lived her whole life in and around Barmouth. Her love for the
lish language, and English literature was nurtured by a wonderful school
her, who – and Norma dwells in the reflected glory of this fact - also
ght Philip Pullman. Leaving school earlier than she would have liked, but
several 'O' level successes to her name, Norma did a secretarial course,
several local jobs, got married, had three children, helped her husband in
business, and also managed to run a small shop. However, dramatic
ring problems, followed by an unsuccessful stapedectomy operation on her
ear threatened to end Norma's working career, until the mid 1980s when
GP offered her a job as a receptionist, and later Practice Manager. Since
Norma has worked for the North Wales Health Authority and Gwynedd
Anglesey Local Health Boards in various NHS roles, including, latterly,
of Operations Manager for the Out of Hours Service. She completed her
ters degree in Health Service Management in 1999. From childhood, the
the Mawddach River, sailing, and all things nautical have flowed through
ma's veins – they still do.

29

The Sweet Taste of Success

ate Marshall smiled to herself as she parked in the visitors' car park of
ITC's sprawling office complex. None of her colleagues could believe it
n she told them that she had landed an interview with the Vice President of
of the UK branch of one of the world's top IT and Business Solution
panies. What a coup it would be for the company if she could win this
unt! Her future at the Recruitment Agency would be guaranteed, not to
tion the handsome bonus in it for her. Stepping out of the car, she picked
er briefcase, strode confidently into the building and approached the
ption desk.

lo, I'm Kate Marshall, I have an appointment with Mr Andrew Jackson at
. I'm a little early'.

shing a smile, the receptionist lifted the telephone receiver and, with a
ectly manicured finger tapped out the extension number.

r Jackson will be with you shortly' she smiled again, offering a visitors'
e, 'Would you like to take a seat, Dr Marshall?'

ank you, but may I use your ladies' room first?'

lowing the directions Kate made her way towards the ladies' toilets. She
ined her size 12 figure in the full length mirror, smoothing down the skirt
r suit. An extravagance, she knew, but now that she was earning well, she
to look the part. A quick brush and shake of the head and her lustrous

brown hair looked perfect. Touching up her lipstick, she quietly ran over her opening lines before returning to the reception area and sinking into the deep leather seats in the waiting area.

It was hard to believe that the good-looking man who strode towards her with his hand outstretched was the Head of Tax of this prestigious organisation.

'Dr Marshall. Welcome, I'm Andrew Jackson'.

She guessed him to be about 42 years old and 6ft 2' tall; his tanned complexion suggesting that he enjoyed outdoor pursuits. There was a self assured poise about him, a steadiness in the gaze of his grey eyes, and an easy confidence in his gesture. His bespoke suit hung perfectly on broad shoulders brown curls just brushing the collar. But before she had time to dwell on how attractive he was or how nice his smile was, he ushered her into a meeting room.

The small room was laid out in a purely functional manner. A leather topped writing desk and chair at one end of the room and, next to the window, an informal low table and chairs. Pictures of ITC's latest advertising campaign adorned the walls and a clock showed the time to be exactly 11.30 a.m. Offering her a seat, Andrew Jackson sat opposite.

'I've arranged for us to have some coffee, but perhaps you'd like to start and me know how your organisation can help us in our recruitment campaign.'

Clearing her throat Kate launched into her well-rehearsed preamble,

'Firstly, let me thank you for inviting me to tender for this position. I am sure you are aware that MWA is one of the leading organisations in the field of financial recruitment in the South East. In order that we can provide you with just the calibre of person you are looking for, I need to ask you one or two questions.'

Kate continued her questioning to establish specific technical, personality and salary details pertaining to the post. She usually allowed herself up to an hour for the brief, and she knew it was going well when she found herself still speaking over forty five minutes later. The rapport between them had been good and she had got on well with him. Confidently she looked him in the eye

'Thank you for listening Mr Jackson, I am sure Morton Wood Anderton can find you the right person for the job.'

He held her gaze, then with a broad smile offered his hand.

'Thank you Dr Marshall, I am very impressed, however, I would like to think about it. Whilst I am very pleased with what you have got to offer, I do have or two other companies to see so I will let you know. In the meantime, perhaps you will allow me to buy you lunch. We have a very good refectory here.'

Kate could hardly contain her joy. Not a done deal yet, but certainly very promising - and now he was offering lunch!

She couldn't help sneaking an admiring glance at this exceptionally handsome man as they took the lift to the self-service dining room. Power was such a potent aphrodisiac.

llowing him into the restaurant Kate's gaze took in the huge array of fare on
er. Counter after counter displayed every variety of food imaginable. Tall-
ted chefs stood to attention ready to dispense cold buffets, salads, curries
d hot meals.

amiliar with the layout, Andrew Jackson headed purposefully to the hot
als counter and made his choice. It seemed appropriate for Kate to follow;
s was a far cry from the hurried sandwich for which she could normally find
e. She played safe and chose the fish, helping herself to a small selection of
getables and, pushing her tray along to keep up with him, topped it all with a
spoonfuls of hollandaise sauce.

ndrew led the way to a table by a window. Immaculate lawns bordered a
all lake on which Canada Geese circled lazily in the late Spring sunshine.
ling she ought to open the conversation,

ave you always worked for ITC?' Kate asked, taking a mouthful of her fish.
ore he could answer she froze – '*My God what's that taste? What is wrong
h the sauce?*' she thought '*It's SWEET. Oh No! It must be custard. I've put
tard on the fish. It wasn't Hollandaise or Mornay sauce, but ...custard!*'
at should she do? The director had already paid for her lunch, she could
dly take it back and expect him to pay for another. Damn, this could spoil
rything. She felt the colour rise to her cheeks, but, deciding it was best not to
ke a fuss, bravely took a second mouthful. Kate chewed on the glutinous
et fishy mess, it was disgusting. Somewhere in the distance she heard him
wer her question.

o, I started as a marketing graduate with Bovis Foods but I left because I felt
y were responsible for nothing short of emotional blackmail ....'

ut, tell me, Dr Marshall is your background in medicine?'

e swallowed another mouthful. It tasted even worse. Gulping down a slug of
er she smiled weakly.

r ...no, I did a PhD in Pharmacology and Physiology, but got fed up of test
es and lab coats so decided to try recruitment instead' she heard herself say.
is was awful. Here she was lunching with one of the most senior men in one
he world's leading organisations and she could hardly concentrate on what
was saying. This should have been such a wonderful experience. It was a
pid mistake to make, but why, oh why had they put the desserts so close to
fish?

e heard him tell her that he spent most of his time in Paris.
and I've just come back from a week's ski-ing in Chamonix, do you know

, yes, I do' another mouthful, followed by a draught of water. 'I did a season
Chamonix in '94.'

ere followed, between sugary mouthfuls, a conversation about ski-ing. They
both done the Valleé Blanche – one of the most exciting and testing runs in
ope over the crevasses of the Mont Blanc glaciers. They had so much in
mon, they could have talked for hours, but Kate couldn't wait to leave!

More conversation. More fish and custard.

Finally consuming the last mouthful, she pushed her plate to one side.

'What about some pudding?'

'No, no thank you' she smiled; and under her breath ... *I've already had som*

'You've been very kind, but I really ought to get back to the office.'

Back in the car, she sat for a while considering the events of the morning. Sh sighed; sure she had ruined her chances of getting ITC's business, started the car and drove back to the office.

Twenty minutes into her journey Kate remembered she had promised to fee back to her boss as soon as the meeting was over.

Reaching forward, she switched on the in-car telephone,

'Hi, Sean. I promised I'd let you know how things went today.'

Sean's voice came through the loudspeaker.

'No need to tell me Kate, I have already heard from Andrew Jackson, he phoned a few minutes ago.'

'Oh I'm so sorry, it was all going so well and I blew it. Let me explain....'

'Not at all Kate, he was very impressed with your pitch and would like to engage us for his campaign. So impressed, in fact, he didn't feel he needed to interview the other companies. Well done.'

'Oh, really? I can't believe it. I didn't think ...... Well ... I'm delighted of cour That's fantastic!'

'There was one thing I didn't understand Kate.' Sean continued. 'It seemed a bit cryptic and really didn't make any sense at all. He said he was very impressed with MWA recruitment but more with you personally. He said tha anyone who could eat a whole portion of cod with custard and keep a poker f is sure to deliver results! What on earth did he mean....?'

30
The Sinister Sea

The forecasters were right with their prediction of low pressure;
    an oppressive gloom hangs over the harbour.
Gunmetal clouds engulf the sky on this drenched August evening.
Once green and pleasant hills are now shrouded in mist.
Grey on grey on grey.

The heavy current sluggishly flows, and water slackens.
The ebb tide drifts languidly from the shore,
A ripple of protest left on sodden sand.
Listless boats nod their subservient bows,
Trapped in windless doldrums.

Leaves hang motionless on lifeless trees.
Dripping flower heads refuse to move; petals closed,
Too exhausted, too tired to raise their heads.

Darkness descends.
Brake lights glint, and tyres swish on wet tarmacadamed roads.
Street lights shimmer through the drizzle.
A black cat pads through the half light,
A harbinger of bad luck.

In the silent dampness, misshapen figures huddle together
Under bent umbrellas
Against the teeming rain,
    trudging towards shelter.

The perch light flashes its three second warning.
Sailors beware its perilous portent!

Some seek shelter in this stopping place. But;
Still waters can run deep – and deadly.
This deceitful harbour has taken lives as well as saved:
Brave young men in recent times lost in the damnable deep;
Echoing cries of that drowning child still haunt from memories of long
    ago.

View this wretched prospect through a veil of tears.

31
Borthwen Morning

This early August morning I rise and look out.
　　My lovely world is tranquil;
　　　deserted.

Dawn skies cast a pale hue
　on the velvet-quilted harbour.
A lone gull sits, transfixed, on a beach pockmarked with yesterday's play.
　Boats lie dutifully on their moorings,
　　marble reflections frozen in a motionless sea.

The rising sun delivers a wakening glow to the hills;
　their shortening shadows protecting the whitewashed village below.
　　Pink candy floss clouds hang
　　　suspended above the grassy dunes of my childhood play.

The sun rises higher in the morning sky,
　rolling back the quilt of night
　　and coastal caravans stand to attention in the early light.

The morning breeze picks up;
　reflections shudder as colours come to life.
　　An eddy of movement stirs the surface;
　　　the silken bedspread shimmers,
　　　　stretching from its marble slumber.

In the distance a lone figure strides,
　his dog bouncing gleefully through the shallows.

The early train is drawn across the bridge
　as if by an invisible magnet
　　and a solitary jogger plods resolutely by.
　　　The syrupy wake of a paddling canoeist
　　　　laps at the thighs of the wading fisherman.

Flags flap and flutter
　in excited anticipation of the day's play
　　and I watch a ferryman put down his first cargo of tourists
　　　on the opposite shore.

ngrily a cormorant in search of breakfast
ecks across the golden bank.

aspiring seagull soars,
reaming, high with hope.

day wears on and traffic increases;
e dust-van 'dragon' rumbles by
athering up the remains of yesterday.

and breakfasted,
attering crocodiles of tourists wind their walking way,
napping cameras recording memories
  of seaside fun.

shine warms the shore.

dren, radiating gaiety and happiness,
rive with bucket and spade,
eads bent in eager exploration.

ns and dads with shoes in hand
ugh their way through sinking sand.

bing his hands, the ferryman fills his boat again.

32
Safe Hands

'**P**ut a move on girl. We've got a river trip today' called Dad as I daydreamed over breakfast.

Grabbing my jacket I ran across the quay to catch up with him. I longed to s[l] my hand into his but feared this too childish for a twelve year old. Opening t[h] heavy wooden doors of the boatshed Dad reached in and pulled from the shadows a pair of oars.

Clambering down the metal ladder to the dinghy,

'Can I row to the mooring Dad' I pleaded.

'Right-oh! In you jump'

He moved to the stern of the boat. Slipping the leather collars of the oars int[o] the metal rowlocks I felt their familiar smoothness in my small hands.

From the stern of the little wooden boat Dad proudly watched the oars dip [a] rise as I pulled away through the harbour to the mooring, remembering t[o] 'feather' them on the return stroke as I had been taught. Shipping the oars, [I] drew the dinghy alongside the motor boat.

The *Enterprise* was a clinker-built open workboat. A brass plaque displaye[d] the name of the builder 'J Spinks & Sons, Appledore, Devon' on its varnishe[d] hull. I still recall the excitement on the harbour in early 1955 as the goods tr[ain] slowly puffed across the bridge with our new 20ft ferry boat strapped to [a] flatbed truck.

With one leap and bow rope in hand, Dad was aboard, I scrambled after hi[m]

A turn or two of the starting handle, and the engine spluttered into life Making his way to the bow, Dad pulled up the mooring, replacing the rope w[ith] the bowline from the dinghy. Moving confidently through the boat to the ste[rn] he put the engine into gear and, with one arm casually resting on the tiller aimed for the ferry steps.

Once alongside the quay, the first task was to check the fuel. Nicotine stain[ed] fingers unscrewed the brass castellated cap on the stern of the motorboat an[d] sounding was taken with a long stick kept for measuring the depth of fuel.

I loved accompanying dad to work, but going for petrol was *not* one of m[y] favourite tasks. Clutching a carefully counted four and thruppence in one ha[nd] and the one-gallon can in the other I trudged across the harbour to the gara[ge] where the florid-faced Mrs Jeffs sat, legs akimbo at the door. She was alway[s] pleased to see me, but not the most careful of pourers, so I knew to stand we[ll] back as she filled the can, remembering as Dad had told me, to check that a *[full] gallon* had been dispensed.

The trip to Penmaenpool was chalked up on the board outside the shed.

Motor Launch Enterprise
16 mile river trip to Penmaenpool
Boat leaves at 10 o'clock
Returns 12 noon approx.
Fare – 4/-d

ᵉ *Enterprise* was licensed to carry twelve passengers and, as soon as they
ᵉ aboard, we left the quay and made our way through the harbour. With the
ɔming tide running at about four knots Dad opened up the throttle and
nouevred the boat through the swirling currents of the bridge. Once through
ɪs allowed to take the helm and, with Dad's expert guidance, negotiate the
ɪer of the channels while he kept his audience spellbound with tales of the
ʌwddach, some true, others a little ....well ....embroidered.

ᵉ mountains of the Cader range resemble a Giant's head on its side. 'Make
the Giant's nose' Dad instructed above the engine noise, and concentrating
d, I kept the bow lined up with this point until I received my next
ruction. When we reached 'the narrows', the narrowest part of the estuary,
ᵈ took over. Without a word he passed me the boathook, my job was to
ɪge it in the water for a depth sounding.

ɪnding in the stern, legs apart and both hands on the tiller behind him, his
; were fixed on the channel ahead. The boat shuddered and slowed as it
ɪped across the banks. The weight would have to be more evenly distributed.
ɔve into the bow please' he commanded his compliant passengers, and with
ɔcking motion he freed the boat, steering it into deeper waters. I sat quietly
ʲing he would not have to get out and push this time.

ɪnce past the most difficult part we could now relax and enjoy our
ʲoundings. Hungry cormorants spread their wings vulture-like on nearby
Ibanks and motherly mallards paddled past, their frightened ducklings
ɪg one by one to the safety of the river's depths. The passengers watched,
Ibound.

od time was made on the incoming tide and we arrived at our destination,
George III hotel at Penmaenpool, exactly forty five minutes later. Steering
boat round in a semicircle to face the flooding tide, and increasing the
ttle for more control, Dad drew alongside the jetty. Bow-rope in hand I
ped ashore, made fast, and helped the passengers disembark.

ᵉ hotel-owner's wife, Mrs Cass, welcomed us with a broad smile. As round
ᵉr tea-pot, she stood, plump hands folded over her cross-over pinny,
ɪnd a trestle table outside the front door. Pouring tea from a huge
ɪinium pot into thick British Rail cups she offered a plate of Rich Tea
ɪits. No tea for Dad though, he had disappeared inside to the gloomy bar
pint. My job was to stay with the boat.

;s swinging on the jetty warmed by the sun, I watched the waters of the
I tide form unpredictable currents and eddies below. The water gradually

slackened and the boat began to shift as the tide turned, a signal that we shou be going.

I ran up to the hotel and along the dark narrow passage way into the bar. Peering in I jumped as a steam train passed by within feet of the room. The b was plunged into even further darkness as smoke belched in through the ope windows. 'Er...the tide's turned Dad' I spluttered, wondering why he would want to spend his time in this murky gloaming when the sun was shining on beautiful world outside.

'OK I'll be there in a minute, get everyone aboard' he said downing his las mouthful.

With all passengers safely aboard and Dad at the helm we set off for home The engine throbbed past salt marsh herds swishing their tails and lifting the heads in mild curiosity. Past tangled shores of driftwood and weed. Pas shipwrecked timbers and sculptured mudbanks the Enterprise comfortably chugged us on our homeward journey.

Nearing the narrows, a stiff south-westerly breeze came up and the su slipped behind a cloud. With a shiver, I pulled my thin jacket around me, an moved to sit on the engine box for warmth.

'Feeling cold love?' called dad above the noise of the engine. 'Get down in t bow out of the wind then'.

Clambering over the seats I made my way forward and dragged Dad's yello lifeboat oilskin out of the cuddy. Wrapping it round me and pushing the anc to one side I nestled down on a coil of rope. The oilskin smelled of Dad, o boats, of petrol and sea salt and I began to feel warmer in my make-shift nes The sound of waves lapping on the hull and the throb of the Stuart Turne lulled me into a happy semi slumber.

Opening my eyes in what seemed like only a few minutes, I was surprised t see that the Clockhouse was already behind us. Time to get back to work a Barmouth Bridge loomed into view. I leapt up, bow rope ready as we weave our way through bobbing boats back to the quayside.

With two half hitches, I made fast the rope to the metal ring on the ferry st as one by one the passengers disembarked with smiles and laughter. Dad, w one hand firmly on the gunwhale to steady the boat offered the other to hel them ashore.

After countless goodbyes and shaking of hands, with thanks for a wonderf trip and promises to return next year we walked back home for lunch. A litt scruffier, a lot hungrier, but much, much happier as I pocketed a shiny sixp - my reward from a grateful passenger.

argaret Ashby

rgaret, from Birmingham, was married to a wonderful naval man, Allen,
forty-three years, and has consequently lived in the many different places
t navy life dictated. On Allen's retirement from the navy, they moved to
l-Wales, near Welshpool, where they set-up their tearooms and restaurant
ch they ran together for many years before moving to Barmouth.
rgaret and Allen brought up four beautiful daughters, who have produced
them nine happy grandchildren and one special great grand-daughter:
e-Leigh. Margaret claims that for all her life she has been a 'Jill of all
les, but a master of none'. Nevertheless, she has written children's stories
ier life (a collection of these is planned for publication in the near future),
" has now entered into a new phase in her writing career which encom-
ses poetry, prose and short stories.

33
C.C.T.V

S mile, says the camera on the wall
        Why?
Have I done something wrong?
    So I look up again –
        Oh, how I wished I hadn't.

I begin to sweat.
    My heart is beating fast.
        Is the camera picking all this up?
            Please stop looking.

I have gone out of the shop now.
    My heart slows down.
        I wipe my face, and I feel fine.

No more cameras, please.

34
The Elements

From the shelter I look out to sea.
    The heavens open up, and the sky is alight
      as lightening strikes across the waves.
        Here comes the thunder – so loud.

I become mesmerized, and cannot go home.

As the sea, with such force, is thrashing over the sea wall,
    the colours, the sounds, the feel of the wind in my face
      makes my heart race, and the adrenalin flow.
        I keep thinking to myself,
          what power this world has.

At the moment it's like a quarrel, up high and below.

As I watch the lightening it becomes so bright across the sea
    it's as though the thunder is saying,
      'I can bang louder. Listen to me.'

Suddenly, the wind becomes stronger; the waves higher,
    racing over the sea wall,
      leaving pools as they draw back.
        Looking into the pools, I see a rainbow.

Just for one second it's like a symphony;
    the music of the elements saying,
      'I'm here. Just listen.'

35
The Unexpected

Vhen my friends and I arrived at the club, Gail rang the bell. We waited a while, then the little grille at the top of the door opened. I saw his eyes. as like looking into his soul. I felt scared.

e you all coming in, or what?' he asked.

s,' my friend said.

vasn't sure whether to stay, or go home.

ddenly he caught my eye; trying to look away was hard.

me on,' said Gail, and gripped my hand just as the door opened. The man ped to the side, and in we went.

t I could feel his eyes follow me no matter where I went. My mouth felt dry. hairs on the back of my neck seemed to rise, so I turned around. There was ual impact. I could not turn away. What's going to happen next? Looking at made me feel angry; he seemed larger than life; he looked like he was ing a statement with his eyes.

you want this drink?' asked Gail.

oking at her, I felt that I was in the wrong place, at the wrong time, sitting t to my friends, enjoying the jokes, and sharing little bits of gossip and hing out load. My mind kept repeating – *leave.*

ere was a tap on my shoulder. As I turned there was the man, his eyes ning to pierce deep into me.

ould you care to dance?'

s.' I replied without thinking; not wishing to spoil the jollity of the group. mped up, pretending to be lively. As we danced he asked what I did for a g, where did I live, and as I answered he came closer. 'Please end the e', I thought.

ng a little lost, and a bit angry, I wanted to flirt, act sexy, but I couldn't. As nan looked at me I tried to look cool. Perhaps the man thought I was naïve. time had come.

nat do you have to say for yourself?'

oked into his eyes. Oh yes, you could definitely see his soul.

ell , little sister, what are you doing here?' he said, evading my question.

that all you have to say,' I asked, 'I think this question is for me to ask - re have you been? After all, *you* left mom, and us kids ten years ago. I am hild; we had to grow up quick thanks to you, so there is no answer to your tion.'

m so sorry,' he said,' please talk to me.'

, it's a little late for that, maybe in the future, but not now; 'bye dad.'

alked back to the table, picked up my coat, and left.

side, I started to shake. Did that really happen....

36
Mountains

S ome people may say mountains have no character.
        I do not believe that.
On a sunny day look how bright they are.
    If you listen closely they seem to be calling,
        'Come on up, I would really like to see you.
Please tread carefully on my carpet so green.'

'Look around , see all I have to offer;
    The high trees, bushes,
        the wonderful smell of the heathers.
Feel the grass between your fingers.
    Look at the colours.
        How can you refuse?
            Today is a good day for me.'

'Come tomorrow if you like.
    It could be raining, windy or both.
        Mist may be rising across my tops.
            But please come and call on me.'

'Friday, it may be late snow is forecast,
    also blizzards; actually near freezing;
        but don't worry, just dress in warm clothes.
            I will take care of you. '

'Do not forget to carry a stick,
    it might save your life.
        You don't want to slip on the ice under foot.'

Remember, mountains have moods just like us,
    so you could say
        that mountains *do* have characters.

37
Place of Happiness

iving in the town there are not many places that are peaceful. We have
parks, but that's not the same.

eryday, when I was young, I fetched some of our neighbour's errands. One
I was asked to deliver a parcel to this old man's sister. It was a bus ride
y from the town.

f I went.

en I found the house, it looked rather large. As I walked up the long drive,
only sounds that I could hear were the birds singing, and the sound of my
on the stones and gravel. I knocked on the door. No-one answered, so I
ed round the house, and knocked on the back door. Still no-one answered.

rned round; there was a gate. I opened it and walked on through. There,
re my eyes, was an arch. I walked under it and looked around. It was so
tiful. Large trees were everywhere, and the most colourful flowers you have
seen.

alked further into the garden.

the centre there was a very big oak tree. As I looked at it I could see the face
old man carved into it. I started to walk away but the face followed so I
t the other way, and still it was watching me. I wasn't scared at all. I sat
n. I felt at peace sitting by the old man in the oak tree. I listened to the wind
ing, and the sound of the trees swaying. I felt as one with them.

wly time passed, the sun was going down. I opened my eyes because I could
someone watching me. I looked at the house. There was the lady who
ed the place. She was smiling at me. I got up, dusted down my skirt, and as
lked over to her. I thought I heard the old man in the oak say,

me back soon.'

as the happiest day of my life.

w I am older. I live in the house, and every day I go and talk to the old man
e oak. The smile is still on his face; and mine.

neday, someone else will feel this peace and inner tranquillity.

38
The Land

Lying on this carpet of grass, I move my hands about me;
How soft it feels.
With my eyes closed, I listen to the sounds all around.
    A cricket hops over my feet;
        I jump up and smile; there he goes.
I lie back down on my soft carpet of grass;
    Close my eyes again.
With the sun sparkling through the trees,
    The shadows gently sway over my body.
I look up; the leaves are starting to fall;
    Autumn is on its way; summer is almost gone.
        and I sigh, it's time to go.
Who knows what tomorrow will bring?

39
Contentment
- to my sister

s I sit on my bench in the garden, drinking tea, I realise how lucky I am to
be watching the clouds drift by, to hear the birds sing their songs. And I
ember the night before. How different things seemed then.

stead of going to bed and feeling the same as every night - just lying there
ving for sleep to come - there I was with my eyes closed; they seemed to get
eavy. I could not open them. Somewhere deep within my dreams I heard a
e in my ear say,

me, give me your hand, we will go for a walk.'

seemed so right, that I gave him my hand and we drifted off together. I
d smell flowers and hear the river as we walked. I remember looking up at
water flowing over the mountain into the stream below,

.' said the man, 'Put your feet in the clear cool water and relax.'

ho are you?' I asked.

m your guardian angel. When you call, we angels are there; right beside
but people do not always remember that, so do not be afraid of me. We
ls do not give life, but come when we are called. Take a look around you
see what beauty the Lord has made; not only the world but most
ortantly YOU.'

it there listening to this angel with a beautiful voice, who seemed to be
ed in a ball of light. As he spoke, my heart was filled with joy.

member where you've been; what you have achieved in this life; look ahead
always remain positive. I will be there when you call. Never look behind
regret because you will miss so much today. Life is for living. When you
aving a bad day, just call. I am always there. You may feel the touch of my
l on your shoulder, or even see a feather. Pick it up, Then you will
mber; I am there at your side.'

40
My Daughters' Gardens

I watched my son-in-law mow the lawn in his garden; moaning about the squirrels digging up his grass. Next day, as I sat with a cup of tea in my ha down popped a squirrel from the tree. It was like watching a documentary on the television. I just sat and watched. He looked all around and then began to scratch at the grass. When he had made a big enough hole ran back up the tree; over branches; collected an acorn, and then ran back down. I was so fascinated; up and up he went branch after branch. Some tim I felt myself holding my hands to my face in case he fell when hanging upside down. It was like a breath of fresh air.

Sometimes we do not see what is in front of us. It's a shame really because i you look there is much going on all around.

Then, when I was sitting in the garden of my other daughter a few day later, feeling the sun on my face; I wanted to lap it up because it's not shon very often this year. Right next to where I was relaxing was a bed of nasturtiums full of caterpillars eating to there heart's content. And on the gr over near the gate a large bush of pretty sedum flowers was covered wit butterflies and honey bees.

And it did not cost me a penny.

elyn Richardson

*yn was born in New Mills, Derbyshire during the Second World War, the
child of a poor working class family. She was a happy child who did well
e school she attended, and at the age of 17 followed her two older sisters
nurse training. Nursing formed the basis of Evelyn's professional life, and
vorked in the health service for 25 years as a nurse, midwife and health
or, before moving into teaching in a further education college. Evelyn has
married to Jack for 48 years, and they have four grown-up children, and
e grandchildren. Retirement has given Evelyn time and opportunity to
lop in many different ways, and her hobbies include reading, gardening,
ing and being with her family. Evelyn is sustained by her Christian faith,
a loving home life.*

41
Nurses

hat do you want to get married for nurse?'
The question astonished me. It was the last thing that I expected;
e some query about managing a home and studying, but not this. I didn't
what to say. Why does any one get married? All I could think of was the
ld reasons, being in love, wanting to be together, it was a long time to wait
I had finished my training; what other reasons did people have? Surely
idn't think that I was pregnant. I would hardly be asking for time off in ten
hs if that was the case. We just wanted to get married and be together;
een months to the end of my training was too long to wait. My hands,
were clasped, rather sweatily, behind my back loosened, and I felt for my
gement ring which was pinned in my uniform pocket.
ve him Matron,' I hesitatingly mumbled.
grey head lifted slightly and she looked at me briefly, with her cool blue
before returning to the holiday chart which lay open on the desk.
sat like this for what seemed ages and, not being able to see her face, I
n't guess what she was thinking. Tired after a long and busy night, I began
l irritated.
ıld see my chance evaporating. What would she know of love I thought,
aritably. Probably been married to her career all her life; would rather sit
office than share her life with a man.
nurse, you can have the time off as requested, but you must realise that
can be no concessions regarding your training schedule'.
ef flowed through me.
nk you very much Matron'.

I was anxious to go; after twelve hours on a busy medical ward and a lon
wait, tiredness overwhelmed me.

'Are you all right nurse?'

I must have looked a bit pale because she told me to sit down.

'Have you known the young man long?'

With this query I told her about our meeting, our subsequent engagement,
even showed her my engagement ring, which I carried, when on duty, pinne
inside my breast pocket - jewellery being banned whilst wearing uniform.
never thought that I would ever have spoken to Matron in such a way, or tha
she would be in the slightest degree interested, but she seemed to be. Afte
discussing aspects of my training following marriage, I left and hurried bac
home as quickly as possible, and then to my bed.

*

I don't know how I restrained myself from smiling, but I just about manag
it. This control I suppose comes from thirty plus years in the nursing
profession. Traditionally it was expected that emotions would be channelle
into practical care and support. It hadn't been easy initially, but over the ye
had perfected it; probably the war years had completed that aspect of n
nursing training, I would never have survived mentally intact if they hadn't

Day after day, during the worst of the blitz there were babies covered in gr
who looked as if they were asleep, but for the layer of thick dust covering th
and choking their lungs; whole families mute with anguish and pain, apart
when a leg or arm was moved, and then only a slight moan or squeak and
flutter of an eyelid.

Later we received the injured soldiers, war weary, coarse, and most wi
terrible injuries which meant that they would never again have a normal li
have jobs , father children or be part of a community. Nursing in those days
a real labour of love. Love; a word to conjure with; yes, even in those days r
of my colleagues had spoken the same words as the young nurse who had ju
left my office. Many married within a few days of meeting; love affairs seen
to grow quickly in the hothouse of war. It always surprised me that ev
seriously ill men were still looking for love. One of my friends was asked fo
date as she and a wounded soldier sheltered under a bed, with only a fe
mattresses propped around them to protect them from the bombs which w
dropping on the hospital. When the rest of us, who could get down to t
cellars, returned, all we could hear was laughter coming from under the be
both were safe! Oh yes love was very much in the air at that time. I was eng
to an airman briefly; but he didn't return from one of his sorties and there
no one else who appealed to me.

For many years I haven't thought about the past, too involved with the my
tasks which come with being the matron of a busy general hospital.

til, that is, a naïve nineteen year old student nurse stood before me
idently asserting that empassioned reply 'because I love him', as a reason
getting married half way through her training. There were no married
ses in my early days, although recently we have started appointing married
nen as part time staff within my hospital.

nat would she do if I'd refused her request, probably get married anyway in
usual two weeks leave most of them have in the Summer.

ne hospitals still will not train married women, but it's getting harder to get
ble candidates to train as nurses. I didn't want to lose a potential staff
e.

night have refused, but when she showed me her engagement ring, that
hed a nerve in me. Her ward reports are good, she took awhile to settle in
nas always been willing and eager to learn, occasionally showing leadership
ities. Just the kind of nurse we want. I only hope that it doesn't lead to a
of similar requests. Still, better this than having to deal with a tearful
nant girl facing life changing decisions about motherhood versus career.
vorries me that a nurse in that situation might try to get rid of the baby, a
where a bit of knowledge can be very dangerous. The last one in this
tion was one of our African students, six months pregnant, no prospect of
riage, and too scared to return home.

career has been, and still is, most satisfying. I've seen the introduction of
piotics improve the outcome of infectious diseases. I've helped to steer
ugh the introduction of the National Health Service; something which at
ime seemed impossible.

ere's still a lot to do and I'm willing to play my part, and hopefully that
g girl will do the same.

couldn't quite disguise her delight when I gave her the whole month off. I
a small twinge of envy as the door closed behind her. This is a different
ration to mine. We were probably too much a product of our Victorian
nts, and not protective of our own needs. In those days it was expected that
u wanted to make a career of nursing then you must remain single. The
that a nurse with husband and children could also succeed in the
ssion was unheard of. That young girl is a sign of things to come.

*

the bus back to my digs I thought about Matron, and how little I, and the
student nurses, knew about her.

wadays I train nurses myself, and I try to give the new generation some
of how things were for me, when I was in training.

ron was an enigmatic figure for nurses in the late 1950's. In all my years at
ospital I never saw Matron in anything other than her uniform. Her dark
dress finished about four inches above her ankles. The bodice was
eetly pin-tucked, and was finished with a small lace collar. She wore a

small lace trimmed cap, and nothing flash or ostentatious was seen about he person.

Her home was a small flat above her office in the older part of the building Nurses wishing to see Matron assembled in the hallway outside her office When the door of the flat open, we could usually hear her talking to her sma dog before she closed the door again. At this signal, the waiting staff stood u smoothing their starched aprons so that no creases showed, and tucking an stray locks of hair behind their ears. The footsteps slowly descended to a sm landing where Matron paused, surveying the group below.

'Good morning Matron,' we would say.

'Good morning nurses,' was the reply, as she descended the final flight c stairs.

A nurse could be outside matron's office for any number of reasons: reporti back on duty after sickness or holiday, confessing to having broken a thermometer, precious in those days and full of mercury, some misdemean such as being cheeky to the ward sister, or other more serious breaches of tl rules and behaviour deemed as being other than what was expected of nurse

Whatever the reason Matron's behaviour was always controlled and reasonable. Nothing seemed to shock her. If you were there to be reprimand she seemed to be hurt rather than angry.

On her ward rounds she missed nothing; word always went round if she w the one visiting; even the patients were on their best behaviour, and seeme pleased to see her and talk with her, polite and respectful even when desperately ill; it was as if the queen herself were deigning to visit.

Matrons set the tone of the hospital. Some were absolute tyrants, and rule place as if it were a minor fiefdom, terrifying all levels of hospital personne Others inspired and nurtured their staff, laying the seeds of dedication ar commitment in generations of, mainly, young women.

*

Back then, it was great to get the time off, and I was impatient to ring my ancée, and tell him the good news. Matron was far from my thoughts as I fe into bed, hoping to get a good day's sleep before another night at worl Hopefully, I wouldn't have another spell on nights once I was married, but I would deal with it when it arose.

42
A Mother's Story

he kitchen floor was a mess. The clean white flooring was splashed with the
congealing blood. The knife lay nearby, the handle smeared and sticky. I
ed at the clock; only ten to two. I looked at my youngest child lying dead at
edge of the blood....if only she hadn't followed me into the kitchen.
t it was just like her; she wouldn't give up. Pester! Pester! Pester! It had
ys been her way, from the moment she was born; and I couldn't take it any
e. Just like him, always wanting attention, always wanting affection,
ting cuddles and expressions of love. He had a selection of pet names for
which I hated, 'sweetie pie', 'little wifey'.... I curled up inside every time he
them.... and she was the same: mummy this, and mummy that, from the
ent she got in from nursery.

e'd been pestering me to help her with a picture she wanted to stick in a
, but no, she couldn't wait a minute. I went into the kitchen to get a drink,
there she was behind me,...

MMY WILL YOU? MUMMY WILL YOU? MUMMY WILL YOU? WILL
? WILL YOU? WILL YOU? MUMMY, MUMMY. MUMMY. MUMMY!
NO! NO!.... GO AWAY!

as then it happened....

knife was in my hand as I turned to shout at her to *GO AWAY!* She didn't,
hit her with it....

was all very quick and silent....She just looked astonished as the knife
red her neck, and ripped through the tissues...

as silent also; there was no noise for the neighbours to hear and report -
s if they could drag themselves away from the TV which blasted forth all
She didn't even make a noise as she fell, just sort of crumpling to the floor.
hat was it, ten seconds or so to take a life that I had created, and to destroy
wn, such as it was.

uldn't undo what I had done.

s would set the whole estate buzzing. They'd love it, all the attention, the
, the people from off the TV, being asked about me. I could just hear them.
ight snob she was, always thought that she was a cut above us.'
t look what she did!'
were a lovely little kiddie.'
uld hear it all, and from them who didn't give two hoots about their own
pretending to care about mine.
d to get away from here.... at least for a night....
re would be an outcry. That I could face. But not the rabble from around
...

I had about four hours before *he* came home.... There were small sums o money around the house which together amounted to about sixty pounds. I this, plus my toothbrush and some condoms, in my bag. It was pouring wit rain; nobody would notice me going out, and even if someone did, with my pulled well over my head, nobody would see enough of me to be able to desc me.

I left the house at quarter to three, quietly and firmly closing the doo listening for the catch to fall. I had drawn the kitchen curtains so that peopl could not see in.

I walked down to the railway station and bought a one-way ticket to Blackp

*

..... They came for me the following day. The chap I was with nearly had heart attack, worried that his wife would find out what he got up to when aw on business!

I was taken back to the police station in my home town, and interviewed by officers there. In their words I was, 'helping them with their enquiries', and named, but everyone knew it was me.

There wasn't much to say really. I did it, and told them so; but they had to on asking questions – endless questions.

From them on it all became a blur; probably I shut my mind to all that wa going on.

I never returned to the house, so I didn't have to face the stares and abuse knew I would get from the neighbours. My husband wanted to see me, but didn't want to see him, so the only time we did see each other was at the tria was conscious of his gaze all the way through it, although I never returned I looks. I suppose he was hoping for some answers, but I had none to give. I c remember anything of what went on. I had pleaded guilty to manslaughter, nobody pressed for a murder conviction as far as I know.

There were never-ending interviews with psychiatrists, all wanting to find why I did it. I couldn't give them any answers that they seemed satisfied wit so in the end, I think they simply gave up. Social workers came and went. T wanted to know if more could have been done to help me with the children; had to produce some kind of report on 'the incident', as they called it.

I was sentenced to several years in prison, which, to my surprise, wasn't a as I had thought it might be. Oh, at first some of the other prisoners we against me, and threatened violence, but in the main they left me alone to g with it. I was no trouble to the staff at all, always quick to obey rules, ar took-up some of the activities open to me. I always admitted my guilt, ar expressed remorse – whatever that is.

I had read somewhere that a lot of male prisoners get fan mail from wom outside; well, as a female prisoner, that never happened to me; not tha wanted it. It just struck me as an odd thing for women to do; it didn't seem

ter how bad the crime, they still wanted to write to the men. As they say,
e's nowt so queer as folk. Lots of people have asked me why I killed her,
I can honestly say I don't know myself. I never liked her, from the moment
was born, even though we had planned to have her. I even tried to
stfeed, but couldn't. I took her to be weighed every week; she had all the
unisations; I took her to play-group. All the things that you're supposed to
I did, but it couldn't make me like her. I think she knew it, and that was why
always wanted me; and it was this that I couldn't bear.
th all honesty, I can say that I didn't plan to hurt her, and I regret what I
every day of my life. Maybe if the knife hadn't been there I would have just
hed her away, like I usually did – life is full of maybes, isn't it?
s nearly time for my release. I've paid my debt to society, and I'm now
ned fit to resume normal life.
at kind of normal life can a woman like me have?

43
Moonbow

L ast night I saw a moonbow,
    a pale arc of light in the western night sky.
        The mundane droplets of a dull autumn day transformed
            by a vivid, full moon.

A dangerous enchantress,
    pulling the eye away from the sinuous road,
        following my path,
            always tempting me to gaze into her beauty.

Who else has witnessed this strange sight,
    and has been moved to depict it?
        Would Constable or Turner have attempted,
            or been inspired, to set it down?

Why no 'Moonbow Sonata',
    or 'Moonbow Serenade',
        to stir the heart?

Shall I compare thee to a moonbow?
    Thou art more lovely for thy fair coolness.
        The penumbra which shadows thee
            enhancing thy beauty and mystery.

And what lies at the end of a moonbow?
    Surely no gaudy pot of gold,
        to be squandered by youths' untrammelled excesses.

More the silver-haired bounty of autumnal wisdom,
    garnered and eked out
        against the coming Winter.

enys Lawson

n in Leigh, Lancashire, and educated at Leigh Girls Grammar School,
re she found her particular strengths in hockey, art, and the boys from
ɟh Boys Grammar School, Glenys made her career with the Inland
enue. Glenys is a successful professional landscape artist, known chiefly
her watercolour paintings, and she has also illustrated book covers
luding this one). She was appointed an honorary member of Stockport Art
ld in 1999. Glenys lives in a chocolate-box cottage in the picturesque
ige of Llanelltyd on the southern slopes of Snowdonia, and apart from
ting and creative writing her pastimes include singing and walking. And
dotes on her grand-daughter.

44
Coming Home

had decided I would stay here throughout the winter before I actually
ought a house, but my lodgings were so cold and lonely that finding a place
y own became more important to me. My requirements were modest, a
ll property, easy to maintain for an older lady on her own, manageable
en, and not too isolated. None of my countless viewings yielded even a hint
purchase until I widened my search, and discovered Llanelltyd, as I was
ing back along the estuary from Barmouth, roads empty of visitors, Cader
still and silent in the warm November sun.

rived at the cottage and knocked on its shabby door. At first glance I knew
s going to be home. As I walked from room to room I mentally placed my
sured furniture; Grandma's bedroom furniture in the front, and Uncle
les' grandfather clock snugly in the hall. A lick of paint and the place could
ansformed.

e owner led me outside, and I was struck by the loveliness of the place. The
e walls thick and solid, the back of the cottage built firmly into the hill, and
front the stream was calling me to stay. In the distance my beloved Cader
turning pink in the late afternoon sun.

vas only then that I really looked at the owner for the first time. A tall,
ly man with large hands and feet, and soft deep voice, stood awkwardly
re me. Maybe he sensed that he had, at last, made a sale.

y do you want to leave this place?'

wife died ten years ago and now I want to move closer to my daughter.'
sadness hung between us. My mind raced. 'Help, I hope he's not going to
I'd seen enough tears to last a lifetime, and, besides, I'd a bucketful of my
to shed. 'Distract this guy, quick.'

ɔk, you've got roses flowering in November. How wonderful.'

He smiled, stepped forward, broke the stem of one perfect bud, and handed it to me. And so our romance began.

It was not long before Ted asked me to move in. Try before you buy, you might say.

But my cottage had a ghost. Ted's wife filled every room; her memory held fast in his mind; his daily visits to her grave evidence of a pain that gave him no rest. He had lost his loved one, and I was no substitute. I knew I could not hold him.

We had six all-too-short months together before he moved to Rhyl. As he walked away there was a spring in his step I'd never noticed before. He was going to start a new life near his only daughter and granddaughters. He left taking his ghost with him. Disappointment and loneliness almost overwhelmed me. Strength came from the new found friends and welcoming neighbours; and the beauty of the countryside was balm to my soul.

Years have passed, and the cottage is quite changed now. I have made it my own. It is my haven of peace in the most beautiful place in the world.

Now, down the road, overlooked by the majestic range of Cader Idris, and guarded by an old yew tree, Ted and his wife lie together, at last.

I don't disturb them.

45
A Fishy Tale

was my habit to go to the bridge each evening. In winter it was usually
deserted, but at other times you were almost certain to see someone with
om you could pass the time of day. Often it was one of the locals walking
r dog, or a chance visitor bemused at their good luck in finding such a
uresque place.

mmer and early autumn brought the salmon fishermen. They would huddle
roups on the bridge, exchanging their fishy tales, each one better than the
before. Their raucous laughter, drifting over the water, made me wary.
y'd fall silent at my approach, before casting me a too loud 'Hello there,
id evening'. I'd hurry past, head down, hoping they wouldn't try to hold me
k with a word or, worse still, a look.

e lived here eight years so I know most of them by sight, of course. Many are
rly and retired. They have fished all their lives with long hours of stealth
patience, and are resigned to their fates, and their disappointments. A few
younger; they are the ones who hurry along the river, urgent, strong with
ose, returning with eyes as glazed as the dead fish in their deep pockets,
with smug satisfaction twisting their tight mouths.

ey are still here again this year, I suppose; most of them; those who have
ived the long winter. But I don't go there any more, at least not in the
ing. They'll all be gathered there to relate their stories.

n't go because I'm afraid to see him again – that fisherman who lured, and
ht me. He will tell how he played me long, and hard. I rested in his
nth, and felt safe. He held me, and stroked me, and told me he loved me,
I believed myself happy. But I was not the catch of his life, and he let me
There was better.

healed, and well, and free; but I'm scarred, and scared; and I don't think
e going down that river again.

46
Brushing Through Life

I know it is the oddest thing to say,
   but my brushes are the latchkeys to my soul.
Do I mean soul?
   It's a rather hackneyed word that – soul.
I mean that part of me that's deep, deep, deep within.
   But where within?
      It doesn't live in my heart, or in my head,
         or even in my mind.
I suppose it's nowhere really,
   and yet it gives me right of entry
      through my silent brushstrokes.
It's a sort of nothingness that is, in truth, my everythingness.
It's the real true me;
   the bit of me that feels, yet hides, life's anguishes and pains,
      and relishes life's loves;
and enjoys the enlivening tones and subtle shades of life itself;
   but yet bears no shackles to the fickle finiteness of life;
      and, for some curious reason, has taken a liking to my brushes.
The raw sienna darkness it paints beneath the arches
   of the bridges in my sunlit images
      is the resting place for the shadows of my life.
The sharp and direct lines of sunlight
   slanting between the leaves of the trees
      are my life's guiding precepts.
Wide and heaven-reaching cerulean expanses
   extol the vastness of my life's scope,
      held in check from time to time by clouds of purest titanium.
And minute daisy-details mirror quietly the many tiny delights
   that sit in life's unseen and unexpected hidden crannies.
The stream, which courses its way beneath the bridge,
   and by the burnt sienna banks that bind the good earth close,
      sees all,
         and is an envoy of the palette-keeper himself.
And when it is the madder that the brushes opt to place upon the canvas,
   my heart sings
      in pure and rose-clad contentedness

[written jointly with Richard Paramor]

⁄lvia Vannelli

via was born in a Derby hospital during the confusion of an air raid. She
s born two weeks late. Lateness and confusion have figured largely in her
ever since. Sylvia's childhood was enhanced by a mother, who taught all
nursery rhymes, read and told stories, engaged in games of make-believe
d enthralled her children by her readings and recitations of poems; and for
ince, by a father, who discussed politics, ethics, social and current affairs
ost daily, with astonishing energy and enthusiasm. Childhood was bathed
language, its power, complexity and beauty. Sylvia's first 'must have' item
s a desk. She was thrilled to be given one as a seventh birthday present and
ted at it she started her first book, 'The Adventures of Cherry Gay'. Sadly
story stalled at around the 7th page of a children's exercise book, in the
'dle of chapter 4. In spite of wonderfully encouraging letters from Uncle
:, of Children's Hour Radio fame, and during her adolescent years, gentle
generous letters of rejection from the BBC's 'Afternoon Story' team, Sylvia
not pursue her intended path as a full time professional writer. Sixty five
rs old this year, these are Sylvia's first published words since college days.
an ambition finally realized, even if rather late.

47
In Control

ulphurous traffic fumes hung in the air. There had been no rain for several
weeks, and dust was everywhere. The afternoon was sultry and overcast.
nder threatened.

ds of sweat stood out, large, on the nape of Gary's bull neck. Sweat trickled
n his back, along the channel running between his shoulder blades, The
fluid stained his red tee—shirt black. The tee—shirt strained across his
orals and the sleeve ribs dug into his biceps, leaving white indentations in
anned skin. Gary wished that he had not grabbed the denim jacket from the
of the settee as he had rushed from the flat. Hooked by its loop over his
finger, and slung over his shoulder, it was a burden in the heat.

y strode jauntily, across the bare asphalt in front of the flats and entered
lley. It was flanked on both sides by wooden garages. Weeds grew across
oorways of some; on others paint peeled and hinges rusted. Violets grew in
y spots between the weathered structures and, in places, dainty tri-
ured heartsease forced themselves through holes in the small concrete
ns in front of the garages. On either side of a ridge of grasses running the
h of the alley was a narrow band of compacted earth, overlaid with sparse
el. Each strip was a car's wheel wide. Gary walked in one of these ruts.

He was out of the line of vision of the tower block now. The alley was deserted he could afford to relax his pose ever so slightly. His pace slowed. He stared hard at the gravel which he disturbed with his white trainers as he walked. The hems of his tight stonewashed jeans gathered a powdering of dust. As he walked, Gary brooded.

The alley curved sharply and came to an abrupt end. Gary turned right into the main road which ran through the estate. From back gardens and side roads came children's voices, sometimes aggressive, often aggrieved, piercing the air. On a front path two youths tinkered with the innards of a rusty banger. Vapours shimmered above the hot metal. Small, black, rainbow-streaked pools overflowed and trickled down the path. The revving of the engine followed Gary down the road.

He had been born not far from here. But the house he had grown up in had been demolished. Town houses had been built on the site. Most of Gary's family had moved away, but he liked it round here. He liked to be near his mates. On Saturdays they went to the match. Blue striped scarves proclaimed their allegiance as they walked together, straggling across the road, down to the St Andrew's ground. There they chanted and yelled. Afterwards they had a pint together.

Gary had grown tired of living with his in-laws. After the baby was born, with three of them in the back-bedroom, they had been even more cramped. Many of his contemporaries on the council's waiting list had been offered places on the outskirts of the city. So when the offer of a flat finally came, and the flat was on the estate, Gary was relieved. He considered himself lucky.

By the time he reached the entrance to 'The Cartwheel' Gary's inner turbulence had abated. It was a relief to feel the certainties returning. It was almost as if nothing had happened. Even so, he felt uneasy about going into pub in the afternoon. He was very careful about the amount he drank, rationing himself conscientiously. Nothing must interfere with his fitness regime. Normally, only on match days, holidays, birthdays and at Christmas did he allow himself to relax his rules.

He worked at his weights every day. He was proud of his bulging biceps, with their rope like veins. He was proud of his capacity to push himself, to extend limits of his endurance, He was proud of his control.

Pausing in the pub porch Gary squinted into the glass of the door, trying to catch the image of himself. But the light was wrong. He could see only his close cropped head, and his bulky outline. He contented himself with running his hand across his spiky hair.

At first Gary thought that the pub was empty. He was disappointed. He needed company. While he waited for the barman to pull his pint, Gary leaned with his back to the bar and scanned the room. It was large and rather bare. The floor was smeared with spilled beer mixed with cigarette ash and dust from the street. The windows were small and set high up. The lights were on. They were very bright. Opposite the bar, a few iron tables stood in front of orange l covered benches.

und to the side of the bar Gary spotted two members of the football crowd, called out to them, pleased. He knew he would not need to say much. They ld recognize that he had woman trouble and, with few words, would pathize. They would understand how it was. He paid for his drink and ching the glass in his fist, he crossed over to the benches. As he approached, two men nodded and smiled. They made space for Gary to sit between them.

*

n the ninth floor a door slammed. A young woman emerged onto the way. She was very thin. She tried to hurry but her movements were ward. The clatter of her spike-heeled shoes bounced back, amplified, from concrete balustrades. She stumbled down the stairway, hampered by the t black skirt. A small girl clung to the woman's hand and struggled to keep the steps too high for her stumpy legs. The child's face was smudged with , where she had rubbed her fists to clear the tears. She seemed bewildered. woman paused to brush the long black hair back from her face. She was ly pale. She shook. An eye was almost closed by puffed up flesh. A livid welt ed on her cheekbone. Blood congealed on her mouth. She reached ground l and struggled forward across the asphalt, listing to one side under the ht of a large sports bag slung across her shoulder. As she passed the ish bay, she dropped the keys of the flat into a bin.

48
The Void

A solitary woman sat on the cliff top; still.
Waves broke themselves on the rocks below. Their water spewed back
into the sea, reformed, hesitated, and battered the cliff wall again; and again
and again. It was nearly high tide. Water boiled furiously around jutting
remnants of granite, not yet submerged by the advancing water. The rhythm
the sea hypnotised, thundering forwards, sucking back, hissing and roaring
Strangely, it both exhilarated and soothed.

Chloe sighed, deep in thought, shoulders bowed by the weight of decisions t
be made. Should she go to live in Australia to be near Sonia? Life had been
bleak since Sonia had emigrated. And now there was a second grand-child on
the way. But she couldn't focus on Sonia. The photograph floated to the surfa
again. The image was never far away.

Each day, for twenty-five years, she had looked at the photograph of Ben, h
dead husband, absorbing his essence, feeling the springiness in his thick dar
curls, marvelling at the lustre as light played on the dense blackness, her fing
wandering through the strands around Ben's temples and behind his ears
Sometimes he pulled away a little; her touch was so light it tickled, he said
Sometimes the memories were so vivid that Ben was able to make love to he
and her orgasms were strong and real, his smile dreamy, satiated.

Then, something changed; everything changed.

On what would have been Ben's sixtieth birthday, a few weeks before th
twenty fifth anniversary of his horrific death, Chloe saw, really saw, the phot
she'd been looking at these years. And Ben was not there. This was not th
image of the sixty year old man Ben would have become, had he lived: husba
of her fifty-five year old self.

What she held an old piece of paper with a picture, remote, static, a momer
the past captured, lifeless.

One Sunday, in the garden of remembrance, where she had her weekly tal
with Ben, sitting on the handsome wooden memorial bench with his name o
it, there was nothing to say. She sat staring at the patch of grass which cover
the urn, and no words came. She began to wonder if the urn was still whole.
couldn't remember how deeply it had been buried. She saw the urn smashe
open, by the weight of the earth above. She saw the worms and the slugs an
the earth dwelling beetles gliding and scurrying among the pieces of broke
pottery, feeding on the ashes. Chloe saw Ben, now new earth, and knew he w
gone from her. She never returned to the garden of remembrance. There wa
now no one to talk to.

The nightmares had been bad again in the weeks since Ben had gone.

112

ney always started with the sound of rushing wind, the scorch of the skin
m the hot air, the choking smoke. Charlotte, her hostess, calm, dragging her
side, still dazed with sleep. And then the sky glowing crimson as the flames
m the trees crept towards the wooden house. The smell of burning, burning,
l the squeals and yelps of the fleeing forest creatures breaking through the
r of the advancing fire. Charlotte, frantic about her dog, still locked in the
hen of the wooden house: and the terror as Ben runs back towards the fire.
ar mounts and she's gasping desperately for air as the oxygen is sucked back
) the fire, leaving a vacuum, followed by the enveloping noise of the
ption, and the fireball racing towards her, overwhelming the little wooden
in. She's stumbling, running, silently screaming, before waking with chest
it, sweat and tears pouring.

n the cliff top clouds rolled in now and strengthening wind, blowing in from
north, bit into the flesh. It was time to leave. She had decided. She would
go to Australia.

loe prepared to get to her feet, her limbs stiffened by the long hours of
ness. She stretched each limb in turn, feeling it warm as the blood flowed
ly through her veins. She took off her shoes and slowly massaged each toe
urn, gently, lovingly. She wiggled her fingers and rubbed the back of each
d, enjoying the tug and the friction on the stretching skin.

ruggling to stand, she brushed strands of hair, claggy with salt, back from
face, and hearing the sound of a train on the track behind her, she turned
ards it. There were young faces peering out, regarding her, questioning her
sence she supposed, in this remote place so close to the cliff edge and away
n any path. Chloe lifted an arm and waved wildly. Many of the children
ed back. The train passed and receded, along its cliff side shelf, into the
ance and out of sight.

loe turned back towards the sea. She lifted her arms high above her,
tching, fingers extending towards infinity. The world receded. The seething
er, the feathering plumes of spray shooting skywards, the tangy salt taste on
tongue, and the greying void of the sky were the universe.

e woman paused, for the briefest of moments, and jumped.

ichard Paramor

rn in London just before the outbreak of World War II, and educated at
nity Grammar School in Wood Green, North London, Richard spent almost
entire career in the transport & travel industry. Apart from letters to
nds – which, apparently, many of them have kept to this day – his only
-retirement writing was travel brochures, and one book. Deserting the
vel industry for the last ten years of his career, he became a village shop
l post office keeper on the Isle of Wight. His latest book was released to
ncide with the 75th Anniversary of London's Victoria Coach Station. As well
occasional magazine articles, he writes regularly in the newsletters and
rnals of various voluntary sector organisations. A new collection of his
tings is to be released shortly.

lished books:
 Man's Search Dickens Publishing, London. (1984)
     ISBN 0946204 50 0 (out of print)
llo, Coastal' Venture Publications, Glossop Derbyshire (2007)
     ISBN 13 978 1 905304 10 3
e released shortly:
Changing Scenes of Life Round House Publishing, Barmouth, Gwynedd
     ISBN 978-0-9560394-1-5

49
Village Sunday

tanding, jaunty-angled, discoloured and dishevelled-in-shape, like the teeth
of a cynically laughing crone, tombstones tell their 'here-lies' stories around
e sides of the church, as it looks down on the higgledy-piggledy village
ng at its feet. A congregation of less than a score, including, in the front
, Councillor Wigmore-Wallace and his Sunday-hatted wife, sings with weak
orious fervour, *'Thine Be The Glory'.*

jan like, Mildred Carruthers, chairperson of the Parochial Parish Council,
-time widow of Cuthbert Carruthers - Town Mayor, Justice of the Peace,
School Governor – in her late sixties and who, not-always-silently,
pproves of Councillor Wigmore-Wallace, and more so his wife, stands at
height, with shoulders thrown back and bosom thrown forward; and
inates the singing with tempestuous contralto excesses with which she
rives to corroborate her undoubted closerness than the rest, to God.

ung Jamie, coming on eleven years of age, peers through heavy-lensed
tacles, and, with prayer book held upside down, listens devoutly to all
's said and done. His 'one verse short of a gospel' mind, soaks up all he

hears with naïve and brain-washed innocence, whilst beside him, his needles
guilt-laden mother tries to atone to God for whatever sins she has unknowing
committed, that should have burdened her with this dented child.

Imbued from top to toe with lavender water, Florence Drew's badly and sad
arthritic fingers play upon the organ as they have for years beyond number. b
now, her crippled hands launch unintended sharpened 'Fs' or flattened 'Bs',
and jug-eared Reverend Davy, who's idly thumbing the corners of the pages c
his hastily written, and now spent sermon, cringes, he hopes unseen, and trie
to sing a little louder.

In truth, he's long relinquished God, but cannot bring himself to accept this
truth; his life now one endless rut of commonplace inconsequence. Supporte
by the routines inflicted by the church, and the, oft times feigned, enthusiasn
of his wife, he 'soldiers on'; though 'aimlessly meanders' might give a better
register of his endeavours. Even his love for his wife is now a characterless
mediocrity of modest meals, platitudes, cocoa and the ten o'clock news. They
long since ceased to honour each other with their bodies, and their sharec
vicarage bed is merely now a place of repose from the boredom of life.

Miss Drew offers one final discordant chord to witness the hymn's ending, a
as a great Amen to her own endeavours. The time has come for those sac
damaged fingers to retire; time for services so piously rendered to cease
rendering. And as a damp-squib closure to an uninspired and uninspiring
service, Councillor Wigmore-Wallace presents to this timid, fragile spinster a
leather-bound Book of Common Prayer, to join the other, less well bound
Books of Common Prayer that lie, revered and unread, on a shelf by the winc
in the tiny sitting room of her tiny cottage. Councillor Wigmore-Wallace':
words are brief, as any over-running of the rite risks impediment to his ritua
arrival at *The Swan*.

Mrs Reverend Davy collects the hymnals, and entombs them, once again, ir
the dusty cupboard near the transept door, before checking if, with judiciou
adjustment, the church flowers can do for another week.

Jamie, with bright enquiring eyes contradicting his hollow, simple-mindec
smile, waves vaguely to all, and leaves with his mother, so over-protective o
her son, and over-protecting of herself.

Mildred Carruthers, still with diva-like immoderation, speaks critically of N
Wigmore-Wallace's meagre speech just witnessed, and, within well-intendec
earshot of Mrs Wigmore-Wallace, comments on the demon drink, and the
prevalence of hoi-polloi-frequented places of imbibement – most notably *Th*
Swan.

A handful of others walk with Florence Drew to the lych-gate, and pa
contrived interest as she shows them, with contrived pride, the book with wl
she has become newly, but disappointedly, possessed, but once through th
gate they hurry off to their homely abodes, leaving Florence to walk with lon
step, and leaden heart, to her own solitary and spinsterly quarters; and as sł
passes the welcoming open door of *The Swan,* as it basks in sinful sunshine

glances daringly in at this forbidden territory, but hastily averts her eyes, hurries on, saved from temptation, eternal damnation and the daunting of Mildred Carruthers' wrath.

ryl Beasley, the sometimes-blonde landlady of *The Swan,* laughs loudly h her customers, pretending to herself she's still in her prime, as she ains firmly and forever in her *very early* forties. Sadly, the tight black skirt wears endorses just how harrowing upon the hips come years, and her tight te jumper covers her now sagging body, which has, in times gone by, been aged well and often by many of those now assembled round the bar. She s happily, but bears a brave, much powdered and painted face, to cover her talgic sadness, and yearning for the 'good old days'.

ouncillor Wigmore-Wallace reaches his warm and welcoming heavenly en in *The Swan,* and orders a double brandy. 'My reward for being goodly godly', he says as he does every Sunday morning at this time. He ogles slyly firm twenty-year-old breasts of Ellie the barmaid, as they parade vocatively before him scarcely sheltered by her unbuttoned shirt; and rishly comments that the views inside the bar, are better than those from its dows; and Ellie giggles - dutifully. He knows that however desperate the eaval in his loins, neither is he able, nor she willing, to bring it to any clusion. Her breasts are for another man's delight alone.

g Pete, rugged and dark haired, stands a swarthy six feet three in his kinged feet, and, as with the rest of his muscular domain, his feet are, to e, intimately familiar, both clad and naked. He and his fellow farmer friends h raucously in the adjoining bar, but, through the adjacent doorway, his Ellie's eyes enjoy a million interim and intimate assignations. Soon, he and will stretch lustily within cool, virgin-white cotton sheets, his large, cultural hands, with infinite gentleness, caressing her cool, unvirgin-white ndaries, with she held captive in his cavernous dark-eyed gaze; and as their ies join, thrusting triumphantly as one, God will look down happily, and the bstone-toothed crones in the churchyard will smile, and the village will live n its Sunday sublimity.

50
Conflict, Conflict Everywhere

Throughout the history of mankind there has never been, not from the Pu
Wars to the Somme, not from Gettysburg to Agincourt, not from the bar
of the Tigris or the Limpopo to the poppy strewn fields of Flanders, witness t
such conflict as exists whenever Myrtle Ackstine sets her mind on a new gird

As always, it began with a local skirmish between Myrtle and the bathroom
scales, when the latter looked like moving into four figures; and then ensued
that period of phoney war, when meals at the Ackstine's table began featurin
an abundance of lettuce leaves, until Hymie Ackstine, normally the most
patient of men, banged his fist on the table and said,

'Holy Moses, Myrtle, since when did we become rabbits? Don't you get enou
household allowance to buy proper food, or has all the steak in New York bee
shipped to Africa?'

'Well I read only yesterday in *Ladies' Home Journal* that we should eat lots
salad, so as not to become obese as we start to get old.'

'Myrtle, we've already gotten old, and you're already obese enough for the b
of us.'

Now, it is true that Myrtle Ackstine's proportions are best described a:
'heroic', but that comment, from her husband-of-almost-sixty-years, was
tantamount to a declaration of war. Fortunately, the next day was Friday, s
she would call Bloomingdale's first thing, and fix for a girdle fitting.

Myrtle only ever buys girdles on Fridays. Sunday evenings she and Hymie d
at the Algonquin Grill, so on Mondays she's more aware than usual of the
flatulence which might make measuring inaccurate; Tuesday is her ladie
auxiliary charity day; Madame La Dessous, corsetiere-in-chief at
Bloomingdale's, doesn't work on Wednesdays, and Thursdays is Myrtle's bri
afternoon, so it leaves just Fridays for buying girdles.

The next morning, Hymie Ackstine, well acquainted with the inevitabl
turmoil ahead, threw his golf bag into the trunk of his car, and set off from t
smart East Side apartment block looking onto Central Park, to escape upstat
for a day of peace and clubhouse beer with his friends Bernie Blumenthal an
Solly Kahn.

For Myrtle, the day's conflict started the moment she called down to th
janitor.

'Oh, Mr Kradwic, would you go out to the sidewalk and call me a cab please
I'm coming right down.'

'No, I von't,' said Mr Kradwic defiantly, 'Alvays I am telling you people I am
janitor here, I am not doorman or servant. If you vant cab you call it yoursel'

Myrtle Ackstine was taken aback,

/ell, Mr Kradwic, I shall make sure Mr Ackstine remembers your attitude
en he writes his gratuity cheques next Christmas.'

at Mr Kradwic had long since slammed down the telephone, so Myrtle hung
too, made her way to the elevator for the sixteen-floor descent, and with
ulders back, nose high, and bosom well to the fore, she marched past Mr
dvic's tiny janitor's desk like a latter day Boadicea in full throttle.

ow, Myrtle Ackstine hated waste, and would not normally take cabs. Even
ugh Hymie Ackstine had been vice-president of the Hoffman Stern
poration for thirty-five years come fall, and could have bought her a whole
t of yellow cabs, she usually used the subway from Lexington and 86th near
Hunter Library. However, it seemed to Myrtle Ackstine of late that the
way company had been installing narrower ticket barriers, and the last time
went to Lexington and 86th, she'd had great difficulty accessing the
form.

ry coming through sideways-on,' a porter had suggested helpfully; but a
sing hoodlum had called out,

o chance, mister,; her sideways-on is even wider than her frontways-on.'
Myrtle avowed at that moment never to use the subway again.

he foundation garment department at Bloomingdale's store on Third
nue, is on the fifth floor behind *Fashions for the Fuller Figure*, and Myrtle
shown to a booth immediately, from where she heard, in the next booth,
lame La Dessous, the corsetiere, with French accent as phoney as her name,
ing to another customer.

it Madam, you 'ave such a slim – 'ow shall I say – countenance - you 'ardly
d a foundation garment at all. Well, maybe, just a little puppy fat, that's all. I
seen you in the Daiquiri advertisement in *Vogue Magazine*, you look so
. 'ere, let me show you the latest garment from José Cortez of Madrid;
or Cortez designs specially for elegant ladies such as you, who don't 'ave a
lem – just a - 'ow shall I say - passing phase.'

soon as Madame La Dessous entered Myrtle Ackstine's booth, Myrtle said,
s sophisticatedly nonchalant a manner as she could,

y friends in Paris, France, tell me that José Cortez is THE fashionable
gner in Europe at the moment; I think I'll try one of his garments.'

dame La Dessous said nothing, but slipped her measure around Myrtle's
le hips, and jotted down a figure on her order pad.

xty-eight, ' screamed Myrtle, 'don't be ridiculous. Obviously you're using
tape from the wrong end!'

dame La Dessous remained calm; this was, after all, the usual reaction
most of the Myrtle Ackstines of Manhattan.

dly, ' she said, 'whilst some of us are designed to look – 'ow shall I say –
e all our lives, others must fight, forever, the battle of the avoirdupois, and
or Cortez does not design battledresses for ladies of your shape. 'Owever, do
ret, the fashion this year is for easy-flowing garments that need – 'ow shall
– structure, on which to 'ang.'

Measurements taken, Myrtle Ackstine swept from the corsetry department as elegantly as she could sweep, with such hatred in her heart and odium in her soul that surely Señor Cortez must, at that very moment, be suffering a terrible seizure, and even Madam La Dessous should be feeling a twinge or two of heart-burn.

Severely battle-weary and laden with purchases, Myrtle Ackstine ought not have said to the cab driver,

'Hey, what's the game buddy? You think I was born yesterday? Coming up West side to get to 5th and 86th; - why not go via Niagara Falls!'

'Lady, it's peak time – you wanna change places? – you wanna drive? – OK if not, trust me, this is best.'

' I shan't be paying a cent over the usual sixteen dollars.'

'That's OK with me lady,' said the cabbie with a shrug, and just as the meter ticked over to sixteen dollars he pulled the cab alongside the sidewalk of a street unfamiliar to Myrtle Ackstine, and politely opened the door for her to get out.

Some time later, after considerable altercation, they did pull up outside her apartment block, and she paid the twenty-five dollar, and eighty-five-cent fare but determined not to tip, she demanded the four dollars, fifteen cents change which the cabbie gave her entirely in nickels and dimes, which slid through her fingers as, laden with parcels and bags, she crossed the sidewalk to the apartment block. Mr Kradwic made a point of not noticing her approach, and carried on sweeping an obscure corner of the lobby as she pushed her way backwards through the double doors, and towards the elevator.

'Hello sugar,' said Hymie as she entered the apartment, 'had a nice day?'

'Don't talk to me,' Myrtle screamed, 'going off like that, playing golf all day with your friends.'

'But honey, you surely didn't want me to come with you to buy a girdle? You hate me coming with you to Bloomingdale's.'

'Oh hush up Hymie, I'm not in a mood for a fight. Pour me a .... daiquiri-on-the-rocks.'

'But sweetie-pie, you don't drink daiquiri ......,'

But he hushed up as he'd been told.

'*Holy Moses,*' he said to himself, smiling, *'I've had a good day. Why risk more conflict?'* And he called quietly,

'Oh, Myrtle, honey'.

'For goodness sake's Hymie, what now?'

'Good Shabbos, honey'.

51
Bugger the Bluebells

n the night of the day when Arnie found the sixpence, and we saw the dead
rabbits, we all lay in Auntie Ethel's feather bed saying 'bugger' lots of
es.

e were staying with Auntie Ethel because Mum had gone to the hospital to
ose a new baby, and Auntie Ethel said she would take us to the bluebell
ds. I was six and my brother Arnold was four, and Auntie Ethel was about a
dred – I think – but she might have been more.

yway Auntie Ethel knows everything there is to know, and Arnie and I like
ing with her because we sleep with her in her feather bed, and it sinks down
oft and warm, and she tells us stories about car thieves, and murderers and

ll, we went on the bus to the cemetery, and then walked up the lane from
e to the woods. There were millions of bluebells, and ever so quickly we'd
ected loads to take home, but they went all floppy, so we threw the first lot
y and said we'd pick some more later.

vas really nice in the woods, and we trampled through the leaves and Arnie
over and got his knees dirty, and we walked for miles and miles. Then Arnie
d sixpence on the ground, and Auntie Ethel said it must be his lucky day,
was a lucky sixpence, so he wiped off the dirt with his hanky and put it in
ocket.

en we saw a row of dead rabbits hanging on a tree, and Auntie Ethel said
must have been caught the night before by poachers with guns – but she
't know why they were hanging on the tree, which surprised me a bit
use it's the first thing she's ever not known about.

yway we walked on for quite a bit more, then sat on a fallen-down tree and
sandwiches and tizer. The marmite sandwiches went first because we liked
n best, and Arnie dropped his in the mud, but Auntie Ethel blew the dirt off
he carried on eating it. Arnie was getting a bit tired, so Auntie Ethel said
best get back to the cemetery for the bus home.

walked for a long time but couldn't find the edge of the wood. Then we
e across some more dead rabbits hanging in a tree, which looked very much
the other ones. Then, after ages of walking, we came back to the tree where
had our sandwiches.

tie Ethel laughed, and said how silly we were for taking the wrong path,
Arnie was very tired and started grizzling, and my legs were really aching.
ll, we walked on a bit more, and when we passed the dead rabbits again, we
v we must be really lost, and would never get home ever again, and would
ably die in the woods because even the fish-paste sandwiches, which we
d, had gone by now, and the Tizer had been empty for ages.

Auntie Ethel said not to be silly, and we wouldn't die because loads of peopl
would be coming along that way soon on their way home from work. But I wa
really frightened by then, and the sun started to go in, and the trees were
making long shadows.

Anyway we sat on Auntie Ethel's coat on the ground quite close to the dead
rabbits, and she started telling us about how car thieves used knitting needle
to open car doors, and bank robbers dug holes in the ground to get into the
bank from under the floor, then we heard a noise.

The man collecting the rabbits didn't see us at first, and Auntie Ethel said,

'Good afternoon, can you direct us to the edge of the woods please?'

The man jumped, and dropped the rabbits, and said,

'Well, bugger me! You shouldn't be here, these is private woods and this i
private property'.

Anyway, he told us how to get out of the woods, and we got the bus home.

Arnie said, 'Well bugger me,' on the bus, and the conductor laughed – bu
Auntie Ethel didn't.

It was really nice to get back to Auntie Ethel's cottage because it was gettin
dark, and as soon as we got in we bolted the door and shut the curtains. We
eggs and brown bread soldiers, and some fruitcake that Auntie Ethel was sav
for Christmas.   Then, after a mug of Ovaltine we went to bed – in Aunti
Ethel's feather bed.

Arnie said,

'We didn't pick any more bluebells, can we go back again tomorrow? I mig
find another sixpence'

'No,' said Auntie Ethel.

'Bugger.' said Arnie.

52
Guy

1 a few minutes I shall be dead.

Crouched down in this seat, with my head on my knees, and my hands ching my head, I'm about to die.

1 about to die!

ay it to myself again and again. Why won't it sink in? I am about to die! why aren't I panicking? I ought to be panicking. Why is everything so eerily et? Why this surreal tranquillity? Nothing seems natural. I'm about to die, vhy aren't I panicking?

rist! Of course I'm panicking; every part of my body is pounding; my heart eating; my stomach is as tense as over-tuned violin strings – I think of the rt on Hui Ling's consulting room wall; the chakra points, the energy centres; right now Hui Ling, my solar plexus chakra is furiously verifying its sence in my stomach with those two tightly interlaced emotions, excitement fear.

hat it? Yes that must be it - excitement. I understand now; I'm not afraid of imminent death because I'm excited by it. From childhood, I recall 'Peter ' – 'dying will be an awfully big adventure.' That's right. I'm about to die, it's an awfully big adventure. I'm excited. I am not scared.

ll! Of course I'm scared - I'm terrified - I'm about to die for Chris'sake. d yet I'm unscared at the same time. This isn't how it's supposed to be. Why : my whole life flashing before me? I'm not even perspiring.

rived from my mother's womb, and I am leaving from this tin womb – this 10 first class womb, flying somewhere over the eastern Mediterranean and it to crash. Both events in some ways matching; curled up tight, as I was i, facing uncertainty with fear; but this time I'm aware of my vulnerability; re of my inability to influence what's happening to me.

God's hands'; the words fleet through my head melodramatically. Do I eve in God? On the whole, yes; but at this moment I don't care. This is the this is death; I'm expecting it any moment now. My mind cannot take in hing else. If a door opens into – what? – heaven – then that's a bonus. It's bo big for me to think about. God! I'm scared!

hink back five hours. I'm in the first class lounge at Colombo airport, ing a gin-and-tonic. I've just finished a 'phone call to Guy. Was that to be ast time I was to hear his voice; thank God the line was clear.

es, I'm at the airport,' I'd said, 'the plane's on time, so I should be at throw about five.'

e deep, velvet, unhurried voice that sends tingles to every corner of my v, had purred like a tiger,

'Don't worry, I'll be there, front of the queue, counting down the seconds to the moment you appear through the door, and to having you beside me, longing to be home so that I can hold you close. I've fixed dinner so don't eat too much on the plane'. The excitement and anticipation in his voice surfaced almost bubbling, from within his normally oh-so-controlled self.

'Love you,' he'd said, as we finished our conversation.

'Me too,' I'd replied.

The young Air Lanka stewardess, dressed in the traditional Sri Lankan costume that the airline had adopted and adapted for its uniform, has come to say the flight is ready for boarding. She's caught the end of my telephone conversation, and her gentle smile implies that she's formed an impression of what the person at the other end is like.

'This way please, Sir,' she says quietly.

I follow her. Excited by my 'phone call, I long to tell her that the voice at the other end of the eavesdropped conversation was a man's. The man who had been my partner, comforter, protector, confidant, conspirator, and lover, for more than eighteen years – since I was twenty and he twenty-six.

But now, here I am, waiting to die. Here in this tinderbox as it's buffeted mercilessly by the storms. God; why do you do these things? Yes, I do believe you, just at this moment - please God – please let me believe in you. If I don't believe in you then what's the point; what is the answer to it all?

I'm thinking of Guy. He's all I can think about. My mind wanders, almost indecently, over the image of his body, so clear in my mind. My own body reacts lustfully. I feel Guy's warmth against me; sense the intimate interlock of our bodies; nestle in the strength and security of his arms. Please God, you can't take this away; it's too perfect. Aren't you supposed to be a God of Love?

Crazily, I try sending telepathic thoughts to Guy.

'Please, please pick up this message,' my mind is imploring.

I've got to tell him what's happening. He'll be leaving for the airport soon, it's a two-hour drive, but he'll be early, and he doesn't yet know what I already know. I shall not be there. I shall be dead.

Soon, he will be pulling his white polo-neck jumper over his head – hell! How good he looks in that. Black trousers will soon slip their way along those long strong legs that carry him to his lofty 6ft 2in. Then black brogues. As he approaches the car door, he will turn up the collar of his short black topcoat. His bright blue scarf will flap around his neck. I see the fullness of his, almost sensuously wavy, not quite black hair, with a rebellious lock falling across his forehead, and his deep-set brown eyes, warm beneath neatly trimmed eyebrows. The book he will have picked up as an afterthought, to while away waiting time at Heathrow, will be thrown on the passenger seat.

t just at this minute, he doesn't know what is happening. He doesn't know about to die. He doesn't know how my heart is breaking, as his soon will be.

had been clear that something was wrong. The cabin crew had become, not much flustered, as agitated. Their smiles belied the tension so obvious in r eyes. Their elegant, relaxed manner became slightly stilted and anxious. last course of that strange meal, neither lunch nor dinner, provided by ines between time zones, was being served. With just four other passengers irst class, service was especially attentive. It was as the stewardess was ring my coffee that she had been called abruptly to the galley. bles were swiftly cleared, and glasses, empty or not, hastily taken away. ten seat belt' signs glowed threateningly. The captain made the ouncement, intended to sound controlled, that sent cold shivers of isation around the aircraft - 'Technical difficulties...faulty ine...unscheduled landing'. The word 'emergency' at first avoided; we were eep our seat belts fastened. A sense of unspoken certainty had furtively n.

w strange is that inexplicable light-headedness when flying comfortably ugh the clouds – like the first sip of a cocktail, a gentle release into a magic eality. But now that unreality has a different guise. I'll soon be dead. That ight, both hideously real, yet fleetingly illusory, hovers like Hamlet's ghostly er – there, then not there.

en had come another announcement. We'd flown almost to Athens to burn uel; violent storms were raging across large areas, with little chance of their ting. Although officially the airport had been closed, an emergency landing thens was to be attempted. We'd be landing on one engine; and there were r technical problems too. We were to remain seated, do what the cabin v instructed, and remain calm.

four first class travelling companions have been silent most of time since announcement. The two clerics are sitting separately now, faces strangely , eyes vacant - their dog-collars providing no celestial preference. Are they, questioning God? The late middle-aged American woman is clutching hard hand of her silent husband, and gently sobbing. Each minute seems like an r.

captain has instructed the cabin staff to be seated immediately. the galley, equipment, firmly stowed a few minutes ago, has been thrown , and is being tossed around like the uncontrolled percussion instruments frenzied orchestra. lights have gone out. There is a scream. w dim emergency lights are glowing ineffectively. The plane is juddering tically as if every nut and bolt has become loose.

Sharp objects have been removed from pockets, clothing loosened, spectacl⸢ removed. One of the clerics, embarrassedly, is taking his dentures from his frightened mouth.

Obediently, we are crouching in our seats. At first an uncanny silence had descended, broken only by an occasional hysterical cry ringing out from ⸢ petrified soul. Now a subdued drone, like a humming chorus of people prayi⸢ is becoming quietly audible throughout.

Through the windows the stormy skies are more fitting for mid-night than mid-day. Torrential rain is battering even more manically on the tormented plane. Lightening is flashing continuously. Is that pitch darkness the Aegean⸢ Please God, don't let us ditch into the cold black sea. Yellow lights are appearing, blurred, somewhere in the distance, scarcely visible through the⸢ deluge. Are those the lights of distant Athens?

The captain is speaking.

'Ladies and Gentlemen, we are about to attempt our emergency landing.'

The helpless plane is being pummelled by nature's fiercest wrath. The dista⸢ blurred lights seem closer – now above us, and, as if on a roller coaster⸢ suddenly below us.

Strangely, I feel perfectly calm, save for the uncontrollable tears falling from my eyes onto the knees of my trousers.

I shall soon be dead.

We strike something; we're spinning around, ninety degrees? Maybe a⸢ hundred and eighty? Now all is black. The seat belt is not holding me any m⸢ I'm being thrown. I'm clutching at anything. It's hopeless. Where am I going⸢ Is this it?

Guy, I need you.

…dex

ROUND HOUSE PUBLISHING